Editor
Lori Kamola, M.S. Ed.

Editorial Project Manager
Emily R. Smith, M.A. Ed.

Editor-in-Chief
Sharon Coan, M.S. Ed.

Art Director
Lee Aucoin

Cover Art
Library of Congress

Imaging
Alfred Lau

Product Manager
Phil Garcia

Publisher
Corinne Burton, M.A.Ed.

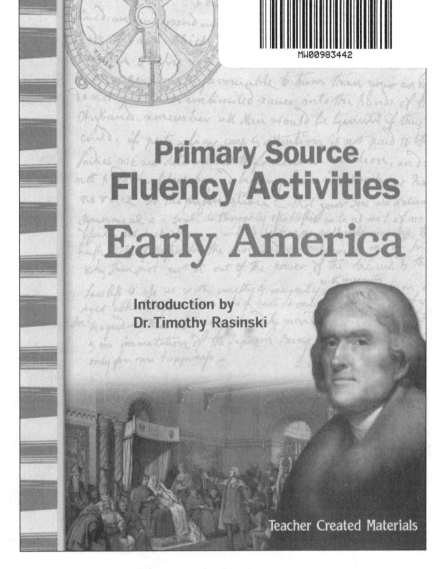

Primary Source Fluency Activities
Early America

**Introduction by
Dr. Timothy Rasinski**

Teacher Created Materials

Author

Jennifer Overend Prior, Ph.D.

Special Introduction by

Dr. Timothy Rasinski, Kent State University

SHELL EDUCATION

Shell Education
5301 Oceanus Drive
Huntington Beach, CA 92649
www.shelleducation.com
ISBN-978-1-4258-0365-0
©*2005 Shell Education*
Reprinted, 2007
Made in the U.S.A.

Table of Contents

Table of Contents (cont.)

Introduction to Teaching Fluency

By Dr. Timothy Rasinski
Kent State University

Why This Book?

This book was developed in response to the need we have heard from teachers for good texts for teaching reading fluency within the content areas. Within the past several years, reading fluency has become recognized as an essential element in elementary and middle grade reading programs (National Reading Panel, 2001). Readers who are fluent are better able to comprehend what they read—they decode words so effortlessly that they can devote their cognitive resources to the all-important task of comprehension instead of bogging themselves down in working to decode words they confront in their reading. They can also construct meaning (comprehension) by reading with appropriate expression and phrasing.

Readers develop fluency through guided practice and repeated readings—reading a text selection several times to the point where it can be expressed meaningfully—with appropriate expression and phrasing. Readers who engage in regular repeated readings, under the guidance and assistance of a teacher or other coach, improve their word recognition, reading rate, comprehension, and overall reading proficiency.

Students will find the texts in this book interesting and sometimes challenging. Students will especially want to practice the texts if you provide regular opportunities for them to perform the texts for their classmates, parents, and other audiences.

So, have fun with these passages. Read them with your students and read them again. Be assured that if you regularly have your students read and perform the texts in this book you will go a long way to develop fluent readers who are able to decode words effortlessly and construct meaning through their interpretations of texts.

How to Use This Book

The texts in this book are meant to be read, reread, and performed. If students do this, they will develop as fluent readers—improve their ability to recognize words accurately and effortlessly and read with meaningful expression and phrasing. However, you, the teachers, are the most important part in developing instruction that uses these texts. In this section we recommend ways in which you can use the texts with your students.

Introduction to Teaching Fluency (cont.)
By Dr. Timothy Rasinski

Scheduling and Practice

The texts should be read repeatedly over several days. We recommend that you introduce one text at a time and practice it over the next three, four, or five days, depending on how quickly your students develop mastery over them. Write the text you are going to read on chart paper and/or put it on an overhead transparency.

Have the students read the text several times each day. They should read it a couple times at the beginning of each day; read it several times during various breaks in the day; and read it multiple times at the end of each day.

Make two copies of the text for each student. Have students keep one copy in school in their "fluency folders." The other copy can be sent home for the students to continue practicing with their families. Communicate to families the importance of children continuing to practice the text at home with their parents and other family members.

Coaching Your Students

A key ingredient to repeated reading is the coaching that comes from a teacher. As your students practice reading the target text each week, alone, in small groups, or as the entire class, be sure to provide positive feedback about their reading. Help them develop a sense for reading the text in such a way that it conveys the meaning that the author attempts to convey or the meaning that the reader may wish to convey. Through oral interpretation of a text, readers can express joy, sadness, anger, surprise, or any of a variety of emotions. Help students learn to use their reading to convey this level of meaning.

Teachers do this by listening, from time to time, as students read and coaching them in the various aspects of oral interpretation. You may wish to suggest that students emphasize certain words, insert dramatic pauses, read a bit faster in one place, or slow down in other parts of the text. And of course, lavish praise on students' best efforts to convey a sense of meaning through their reading. Although it may take a while for the students to learn to develop this sense of "voice" in their reading, in the long run it will lead to more engaged and fluent reading and higher levels of comprehension.

Introduction to Teaching Fluency (cont.)
By Dr. Timothy Rasinski

Word Study

Although the goal of the passages in this book is to develop fluent and meaningful oral reading, the practicing of passages should also provide opportunities to develop students' vocabulary and word decoding skills. Students may practice a passage repeatedly to the point where it is largely memorized. At this point, students may not look at the words in the text as closely as they ought. By continually drawing attention to interesting and important words in the text you can help students maintain their focus and develop an ongoing fascination with words.

After reading a passage several times through, ask students to choose words from the passage that they think are interesting or important. Put these words on a word wall, or ask students to add them to their personal word banks. Talk about the words, their meanings and spellings. Help students develop a deepened appreciation for these words. Encourage students to use these words in their oral and written language. You might, for example, ask students to use some of the chosen words in their daily journal entries each day.

Once a list of words has been added to a classroom word wall or students' word banks, play various games with the words. One of our favorites is "word bingo." Here, students are given a card containing a 3 x 3, 4 x 4, or 5 x 5 grid. In each box, students randomly write words from the word wall or bank. Then, the teacher calls out words or sentences that contain the target words or definitions of the target words. Students find the words on their cards and cover them with markers. Once a horizontal, vertical, or diagonal line of words is covered, a student calls "Bingo" and wins the game.

Have students sort the chosen words along a variety of dimensions—by syllable, part of speech, presence of a certain phonics features such as long vowel sound or a consonant blend, or by meaning (e.g., words that express how a person can feel and words that don't). Through sorting and categorizing activities, students get repeated exposure to words, all the time examining the words differently with each sort.

Choose words from a text that lend themselves to extended word family instruction. Choose a word like "hat" and brainstorm with students other words that belong to the same word family (e.g., "cat," "bat," "chat," etc.). Once a brainstormed list of word family words are chosen, have students create short poems using the rhyming words. These composed poems can be used for further practice and performance.

No matter how you do it, make the opportunity to examine selected words from the passages part of your regular instructional routine for these fluency texts. The time spent in word study will most definitely improve students' overall fluency.

Introduction to Teaching Fluency (cont.)
By Dr. Timothy Rasinski

Performance

After several days of practice, arrange a special time of a day for the students to perform the text, as well as other ones practiced from previous days. This performance time can range from five minutes to 30 minutes. Find a special person (such as the principal) to listen to your children perform. You may also want to invite a neighboring class, parents, or another group to come to your room to listen to your children perform. Have the children perform the targeted text as a group. Later, you can have individuals or groups of children perform the text again, as well as other texts that have been practiced previously.

As an alternative to having your children perform for a group that comes to your room, you may also want to send your children to visit other adults and children in the building and perform for them. Principals, school secretaries, custodians, playground aides, and visitors to the building are usually great audiences for children's reading. Tape recording and video taping your students' reading is another way to create a performance opportunity.

Regardless of how you do it, it is important that you create the opportunity for your students to perform for some audience. The magic of the performance will give students the motivation to want to practice their assigned texts.

Performance Not Memorization

Remember that the key to developing fluency is guided oral and silent reading practice. Students become more fluent when they read the text repeatedly. Reading requires students to actually see the words in the text. Thus, it is important that you do not require students to memorize the texts they are practicing and performing. Memorization leads students away from visually examining the words. Although students may want to try to memorize some texts, the instructional emphasis needs to be on reading with expression so that any audience will enjoy the students' oral rendering of the text. Keep students' eyes on the text whenever possible.

One of the most important things we can do to promote proficient and fluent reading is to have students practice reading meaningful passages with a purpose: to perform them. This program provides students with just those opportunities to create meaning with their voices as well as the wonderful words in these primary sources.

How to Use This Product

General Information

This book contains famous historical texts such as speeches, poems, letters, government documents, newspaper articles, and songs. Each of these primary sources are from the early American period (i.e., exploration through the writing of the Constitution). Activities for each primary source teach important fluency strategies while covering key historical events and people, such as exploring the New World, American Indian tribes, colonial life, the Revolutionary Era, Abigail Adams, Thomas Jefferson, George Washington, and Benjamin Franklin.

Depending on the reading levels of your students, you may find some of these pieces too difficult to use at the beginning of the year. Instead, focus on the pieces that are rewritten or pieces where the original reading level is lower. Unfortunately for students today, we write differently now than the people of the past. What that means for our students is that they often have to decipher very difficult and complex writing just to read a primary source document. This book is set up to help your students be successful as they tackle writings from the past. Instead of just reading the document or letter once and moving on, the students practice and reread the pieces in preparation for authentic presentations. That way, not only does their fluency grow through careful repetition, but as the class discusses the pieces, the students' comprehension improves as well.

Presentations

One of the most important aspects of these lessons are the presentation pieces. The authors and editors of this book have tried to provide you with plenty of ideas. If the idea suggested for a certain piece will not work for your classroom situation, flip through the book and look for other suggestions that might be suitable. The key is that you have the students practice reading the pieces for authentic reasons. If the end presentation is always just to their own class, they will quickly lose interest. Once they've lost interest in the performance, they will not work as hard at perfecting their fluency. You will not see much growth in your students if they feel that all their practice is for nothing.

Instead, be creative and fun as you plan these presentations. Invite different guests or whole classes in to hear your presentations. Younger classes make great audiences if the content is something they are also studying. Keep in mind that many teachers of younger students cover George Washington, Thomas Jefferson, Benjamin Franklin, the Declaration of Independence, and the Constitution whether it is specifically in their standards or not.

How to Use This Product (cont.)

Presentations (cont.)

If you have a hard time finding people to whom your class can present, try to tie the presentations into celebrations or holidays. Some possible times to hold presentations might include: Presidents' Day, the beginning of spring, Mother's Day, Memorial Day, Flag Day, the first day of summer, Father's Day, Labor Day, when autumn begins, Columbus Day, Election Day, Veteran's Day, Thanksgiving day, and when winter begins. Don't forget about celebrations that take place over whole months. Some of these include: Black History Month, American Indian Heritage Month, and Women's History Month.

Finally, try to tie your presentations into schoolwide events. For example, you could have your students add to the school's morning announcements. Or, you could ask for a special part in the Veteran's Day celebration. Rather than holding your own assembly, work with other teachers to hold a Poetry Celebration where students read historical poetry. Remember, your students' fluency will only improve if you make the performances important and authentic.

Reader's Theater

Throughout the lessons in this book, you will find numerous reader's theater scripts. This is an exciting and easy method of providing students with the opportunity to practice fluency leading to a performance. Because reader's theater minimizes the use of props, sets, costumes, and memorization, it is an easy way to present a "play" in the classroom. Students read from a book or prepared script using their voices to bring to text to life. Reader's theater has the following characteristics:

1. The script is always read and never memorized.
2. Readers may be characters, narrators, or switch back and forth.
3. The readers may sit, stand, or both, but they do not have to perform any other actions.
4. Readers use only eye contact, facial expressions, and vocal expression to express emotion.
5. Scripts may be from books, songs, poems, letters, etc. They can be performed directly from the original material or adapted specifically for the reader's theater performance.
6. Musical accompaniment or soundtracks may be used, but are not necessary.
7. Very simple props may be used, especially with younger children, to help the audience identify the roles played by the readers.
8. Practice for the reader's theater should consist of coached repeated readings that lead to a smooth, fluent presentation.

How to Use This Product (cont.)

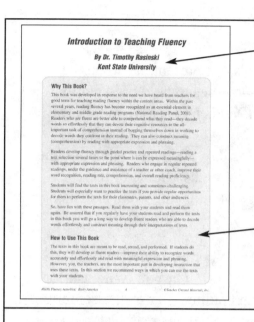

Introduction Written by Dr. Timothy Rasinski

- In a survey conducted by the National Reading Panel, fluency was determined to be one of the five researched-based components of reading. Dr. Timothy Rasinski from Kent State University is an expert on teaching students to become fluent readers. His book, *The Fluent Reader*, is an excellent resource of oral reading strategies for building word recognition, fluency, and comprehension.

How to Use This Book

- Dr. Rasinski's introduction contains important information and ideas of how to use this book with your readers.

Objective

- A fluency objective is included for each lesson. This objective tells you which fluency strategy will be practiced within the lesson. See pages 12–13 for descriptions of the fluency strategies used within this book.

Fluency Suggestions and Activities

- These steps in the lesson plan describe how to introduce the piece to your students. Suggestions for ways to practice and perform the piece are also provided for your use. Remember that authentic performances are very important to ensure successful fluency for your readers.

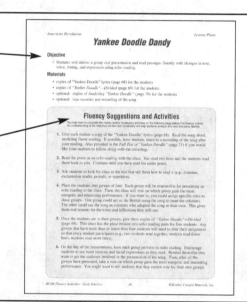

History Connection

- Each text in this book relates to an important historical person or event. Information is provided with each lesson to give you the historical context of the piece.

Vocabulary Connection

- Vocabulary words have been chosen and defined for your use. Introduce the words to your students and have them define the words, or you can simply record the definitions on the board for student reference.

Extension Ideas

- One or two extension ideas are given for each lesson. These ideas are usually fun, challenging, and interesting.

How to Use This Product *(cont.)*

Primary Source Text

- For each lesson, a copy of the primary source text is provided for the teacher. Sometimes, the students will not receive copies of this text. They may only receive copies of the rewritten text, divided reading, or reader's theater. This text is provided so that teachers can read the original document to the students and/or refer to it as they teach the lesson to the class.

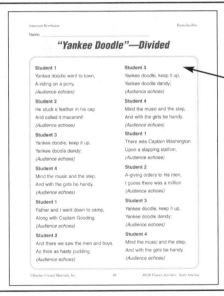

Student Versions of the Primary Source Text

- For most of the texts, the author of the book has rewritten the texts for the students to use. Sometimes, it is simply rephrased in modern language. Other times, the text has been divided into smaller reading sections. There are also pieces that have been rewritten into reader's theater scripts for the students to perform.

Student Reproducibles

- For most of the lessons, at least one of the student reproducibles is designed to help students analyze the text. These are quite often one of the extension activities since they do not focus on fluency as much as comprehension of the piece. If time allows, be sure to complete these activity sheets with your students.

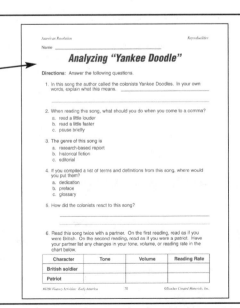

Fluency Strategy Descriptions

These paragraphs describe the fluency strategies taught through the lessons in this book. These descriptions are meant to provide teachers with basic information about the strategies before beginning the lessons.

Choral Reading

Choral reading is when groups of students read the same text aloud together. This strategy has become more popular in recent years. It allows for a lot of reading time by all students rather than single students reading while everyone else listens.

Cumulative Choral Reading

This is a special type of choral reading where one student begins reading. Then, at predetermined points, other students join in the reading. By the end of the passage, the entire group is reading in unison.

Echo Reading

In echo reading, one reader (or a small group) reads a part of the text. Then, the rest of the group (or class) echoes back the same text.

Oral Reading

Oral reading is when the students read the text aloud rather than silently. All of the strategies in this book fall under the strategy of oral reading.

Paired Reading

Paired reading is when two students or a student and an adult read text together. They can either read it chorally or they can read alternating lines or stanzas.

Poem for Two Voices

This type of poem has been written (or rewritten) so that it can be read by two readers. The readers alternate between lines of the poem while sometimes reading lines together.

Reader's Theater

Reader's theater is usually written for three to five students. It includes lines of the text that are shared individually and lines that are stated by all the students. It is like a script of a play, but there are few props and no costumes used in the production of the piece.

Repeated Reading

This type of reading is when the students read and reread a piece to improve upon their fluency. Every lesson within this book suggests that you have the students use repeated reading to improve their fluency before the performance of the piece.

Fluency Strategy Descriptions (cont.)

This chart indicates the fluency strategies practiced within the lessons in this book. Some lessons have more than one strategy marked because students will be working on multiple skills within the lesson.

Lesson	Choral Reading	Cumulative Choral Reading	Echo Reading	Oral Reading	Paired Reading	Poem for Two Voices	Reader's Theater	Repeated Reading
Exploration Log (pages 14–17)				X				X
Sir Francis Drake (pages 18–22)		X						X
Iroquois Poetry (pages 23–27)				X				X
Pueblo Traditional Song (pages 28–32)						X		X
Learning about Pilgrims (pages 33–36)					X			X
Slavery in America (pages 37–41)								X
The Boston Tea Party (pages 42–46)				X				X
Liberty in the Colonies (pages 47–52)		X						X
Declaring Independence (pages 53–60)				X				X
Patrick Henry Speaks (pages 61–65)							X	X
Yankee Doodle Dandy (pages 66–71)			X					X
Paul Revere's Famous Night (pages 72–77)	X							X
Paine's Common Sense (pages 78–82)								X
July 4, 1788 (pages 83–86)	X							X
Preamble to the Constitution (pages 87–91)							X	X
The First Ten Amendments (pages 92–99)				X				X
Arriving in the New World (pages 100–105)							X	X
The Explorer Columbus (pages 106–111)						X		X
Pocahontas of the Powhatan Tribe (pages 112–114)		X						X
Pocahontas and John Rolfe (pages 115–117)					X			X
From Africa to America (pages 118–122)				X				X
Earl of Dartmouth (pages 123–129)					X			X
The Boston Massacre (pages 130–135)							X	X
Remember the Ladies (pages 136–140)							X	X
Jefferson's Reaction to the Constitution (pages 141–146)							X	X
Thomas Jefferson Writes (pages 147–156)				X				X
George and Martha Washington (pages 157–160)				X				X
Washington's Farewell Speech (pages 161–165)							X	X
The Bald Eagle (pages 166–170)				X				X
Benjamin Franklin (pages 171–180)				X				X
The Federalist Papers (pages 181–187)							X	X
Treaty of Paris Boundaries (pages 188–192)				X				X

Exploration Log

Fluency Objective

√ Students will read passages fluently and accurately within a group oral reading activity, focusing on conversational, expressive language.

Materials

- overhead transparency of *Columbus Log* (page 16)
- copies of *Columbus Log Divided Reading* (page 17) for the students

Fluency Suggestions and Activities

You may want to complete the history and/or vocabulary activities on the following page before this fluency activity. An understanding of the historical context and vocabulary will help students analyze and read the piece fluently.

1. Display the *Columbus Log* (page 16) on an overhead projector. Read the two journal entries aloud, demonstrating fluency, as the students follow along. Draw students' attention to the expressive, conversational style used as you read.

2. Read the text a few more times using different reading styles. You could read it like a formal speech or in a short, choppy fashion. Compare the different styles of reading and ask the students to comment on the most appropriate way to read this particular text.

3. Next, tell the students that they are traveling back in time. Christopher Columbus has just returned from his journey to the New World. Columbus wants to be as famous as Marco Polo. (Polo became famous after he wrote a book about his travels to China.) So, Columbus is trying to find a good publisher to print his journal. He wants to find a group of people to read his journal in an exciting, interesting way so that the publishers will fight to be able to print the book. (This means more money for Columbus.) He's invited the students in this class to give public performances of his journal. He will decide which group gets to perform the reading for the publishers. So, students need to work hard within their groups to figure out the most interesting and exciting way they can perform the reading!

4. Divide the students into groups of four and give them copies of the *Columbus Log Divided Reading* (page 17). The text of the journal entries is divided into four parts. A student in each group will be assigned to read each part. The sections of text are leveled so that you can assign students to the reading parts that best fit their reading levels. Reader 1 is level 4.7; Reader 2 is level 3.6; Reader 3 is level 5.3; and Reader 4 is level 3.4.

5. Allow the students time in class and at home to practice reading their parts, focusing on expressive, conversational language. They should have time together as well as individually to prepare for the presentation.

6. When students have had the opportunity to practice reading their parts several times and on a few different occasions, set up a presentation day. Invite someone into the room to act as Columbus (principals work nicely for this). Each group should present its oral reading to the class. At the end, "Columbus" can declare that everyone did such a good job that he can't decide. They're all winners! (Or, if your students enjoy a bit of competition, you can have the class take a vote on which group gave the most energetic and interesting presentation of the material.)

Exploration Log (cont.)

History Connection

Discuss Columbus' journeys as an explorer. Explain that Columbus kept records of his travels by writing in journals. Ask the students why he might have kept records of his travels. During this discussion, share facts from the historical background information provided below.

Christopher Columbus was one of the finest sailors of his time. He hoped to find a shorter route to India, China, and Japan by traveling west through uncharted waters. The trip took longer than expected because Columbus did not know that Earth was as large as it is. He thought it was smaller. He did not tell the sailors the actual distance traveled each day because they would worry about being far away from home. He encouraged his men with promises of riches and fame. He kept a record of his journeys in his logbook.

Vocabulary Connection

Discuss unfamiliar vocabulary encountered in the text. Some possible words are listed below. After identifying the difficult words, discuss them within the context of the text.

- **reckoning**—a count of something, accounting
- **appearance**—how something looks
- **summoned**—called someone or something
- **adequate**—enough of something
- **seaman**—a man who works at sea
- **lay-to**—to hold a ship still by turning it into the wind

Extension Ideas

- Challenge the students to do expressive reading of their own journal entries. Have them write journal entries or select entries from journals they have been keeping. Instruct the students to practice reading their selected entries and then perform them for the class or small groups within the class.

- Have your students locate other journal entries written by Christopher Columbus about his journeys using resource books or the Internet.

Columbus Log

Sunday, 9 September, 1492

This day we completely lost sight of land. Many men sighed and wept for fear they would not see it again for a long time. I comforted them with great promises of lands and riches. I decided to count fewer miles than we actually made. I did this so the sailors might not think themselves as far from Spain as they really were. For myself I kept a confidential, accurate, reckoning. Tonight I made ninety miles.

Thursday, 11 October, 1492

I sailed to the west-southwest. The crew of the Pinta spotted reeds and a small board. A stick was found that looks man-made, perhaps carved with an iron tool. These made the crew breathe easier; in fact, the men have even become cheerful. A special thanksgiving was offered to God for giving us renewed hope through the many signs of land.

About ten o'clock at night I saw a light to the west. It looked like a wax candle bobbing up and down. It had the same appearance as a light or torch belonging to fishermen or travelers who raised and lowered it. I am the first to admit I was so eager to find land that I did not trust my own senses, so I called Gutierrez and asked him to watch for the light. After a few moments, he, too, saw it. I then summoned Rodrigo Sanchez. He saw nothing, nor did any other member of the crew. It was such an uncertain thing I did not feel it was adequate proof of land. Then, at two hours after midnight, the *Pinta* fired a cannon, my signal for the sighting of land.

I now believe the light I saw was truly land. When we caught up with the *Pinta*, I learned Rodrigo de Triana, a seaman, was the first to sight land. I lay-to till daylight. The land is about six miles to the west.

Name _____

Columbus Log Divided Reading

Reader 1

Sunday, 9 September, 1492

This day we completely lost sight of land. Many men sighed and wept for fear they would not see it again for a long time. I comforted them with great promises of lands and riches. I decided to count fewer miles than we actually made. I did this so the sailors might not think themselves as far from Spain as they really were. For myself I kept a confidential, accurate, reckoning. Tonight I made ninety miles.

Reader 2

Thursday, 11 October, 1492

I sailed to the west-southwest. The crew of the Pinta spotted reeds and a small board. A stick was found that looks man-made, perhaps carved with an iron tool. These made the crew breathe easier; in fact, the men have even become cheerful. A special thanksgiving was offered to God for giving us renewed hope through the many signs of land.

Reader 3

About ten o'clock at night I saw a light to the west. It looked like a wax candle bobbing up and down. It had the same appearance as a light or torch belonging to fishermen or travelers who raised and lowered it. I am the first to admit I was so eager to find land that I did not trust my own senses, so I called Gutierrez and asked him to watch for the light. After a few moments, he, too, saw it. I then summoned Rodrigo Sanchez. He saw nothing, nor did any other member of the crew. It was such an uncertain thing I did not feel it was adequate proof of land. Then, at two hours after midnight, the *Pinta* fired a cannon, my signal for the sighting of land.

Reader 4

I now believe the light I saw was truly land. When we caught up with the *Pinta*, I learned Rodrigo de Triana, a seaman, was the first to sight land. I lay-to till daylight. The land is about six miles to the west.

Sir Francis Drake

Fluency Objective

√ Students will read passages fluently and accurately within a cumulative choral reading activity, focusing on correct conversational, expressive language.

Materials

- overhead transparency of *Voyage of Sir Francis Drake* (page 20)
- overhead transparency of *Voyage of Sir Francis Drake Cumulative Reading* (pages 21–22)
- copies of *Voyage of Sir Francis Drake Cumulative Reading* (pages 21–22) for the students

Fluency Suggestions and Activities

You may want to complete the history and/or vocabulary activities on the following page before this fluency activity. An understanding of the historical context and vocabulary will help students analyze and read the piece fluently.

1. Explain that the text for this lesson is a record of one of Sir Francis Drake's voyages. Remind the students to use expressive language when reading with fluency.

2. Display the transparency of the *Voyage of Sir Francis Drake* (page 20) on the overhead projector for all to see. Read the first paragraph, demonstrating fluency with accuracy and expression. Focus particular attention on the use of long sentences, divided by commas. Explain that when reading long sentences, it is important to pause, when commas are encountered, to assist with the understanding of the text. Tell students that this is especially important when reading aloud for others, as they will be doing at the end of the lesson. Demonstrate this by reading the sentence below, pausing at each comma:

   > The 15th day of November, (pause) in the year of our Lord 1577, (pause) Master Francis Drake, (pause) with a fleet of five ships and barks, (pause) and to the number of 164 men, (pause) gentlemen and sailors, (pause) departed from Plymouth, (pause) giving out his pretended voyage for Alexandria.

3. Explain to the students that they are practicing this skill so that they will be prepared for a cumulative choral reading activity. The students will read the text in groups of three. This means that one student will read a line, then another student joins as the first student continues, and then a third student joins in reading with the first two. Have two students help you demonstrate this process with the passage below. (Explain that R1, R2, and R3 stand for Reader 1, Reader 2, and Reader 3.)

   > R1: The FAMOUS VOYAGE of Sir FRANCIS DRAKE into the South Sea,
   > R1, R2: and therehence about the whole Globe of the Earth,
   > R1, R2, R3: begun in the year of our Lord 1577.

4. Divide the students into groups of three and assign parts to the students. Allow the students time in class to practice reading their parts, focusing on expressive, conversational language.

5. Arrange for the groups to perform their cumulative readings publicly to other classes, administrators, or parents.

Sir Francis Drake *(cont.)*

History Connection

Use this information to discuss how Sir Francis Drake worked with Queen Elizabeth I to fight against the Spanish Armada and other enemies of the British.

Queen Elizabeth I hired Francis Drake to take riches from Spanish ships. Drake also explored the New World. After sailing through the Straits of Magellan in 1577, he headed north along the west coast of South America. Along the way he raided treasures from Spanish ships. The gold he took was so heavy that it almost sunk his ship!

Drake continued north and explored the coast of California. He looked for the Northwest Passage hoping to sail east. He did not find it, so he sailed across the Pacific Ocean and back to England. There, the queen knighted him and sent him out on more important trips.

Vocabulary Connection

Discuss unfamiliar vocabulary encountered in the text. Some possible words are listed below. After identifying the difficult words, discuss them within the context of the text.

- **therehence**—after that
- **fleet**—group of ships or boats sailing together
- **barks**—small sailing ships
- **contrary**—unfavorable
- **tempest**—violent storm
- **vehement**—strong
- **wrack**—wreck or smashed
- **extremity**—very great danger
- **afflict**—hurt
- **withal**—with
- **notwithstanding**—however
- **spawning**—producing

Extension Idea

- Have your students locate more information about Sir Francis Drake using an Internet search engine. Instruct the students to try different search terms, such as "Sir Francis Drake" or "Sir Francis Drake Voyages." Have the students write paragraphs of new information they gather about Drake. Then have them practice reading the paragraphs with fluency to perform for classmates.

Voyage of Sir Francis Drake

The FAMOUS VOYAGE of Sir FRANCIS DRAKE into the South Sea, and therehence about the whole Globe of the Earth, begun in the year of our Lord 1577.

The 15th day of November, in the year of our Lord 1577, Master Francis Drake, with a fleet of five ships and barks, and to the number of 164 men, gentlemen and sailors, departed from Plymouth, giving out his pretended voyage for Alexandria. But the wind falling contrary, he was forced the next morning to put into Falmouth Haven, in Cornwall, where such and so terrible a tempest took us, as few men have seen the like, and was indeed so vehement that all our ships were like to have gone to wrack. But it pleased God to preserve us from that extremity and to afflict us only for that present with these two particulars: the mast of our Admiral, which was the *Pelican,* was cut overboard for the safeguard of the ship, and the *Marigold* was driven ashore, and somewhat bruised. For the repairing of which damages we returned again to Plymouth; and having recovered those harms, and brought the ships again to good state, we set forth the second time from Plymouth, and set sail the 13th day of December following . . . .

. . . Not long before our departure, they told us that not far off there were such great ships as ours, wishing us to beware; upon this our captain would stay no longer. From Java Major we sailed for the Cape of Good Hope, which was the first land we fell withal; neither did we touch with it, or any other land, until we came to Sierra Leona, upon the coast of Guinea; notwithstanding we ran hard aboard the cape, finding the report of the Portugals to be most false who affirm that it is the most dangerous cape of the world, never without intolerable storms and present danger to travellers which come near the same. This cape is a most stately thing, and the fairest cape we saw in the whole circumference of the earth, and we passed by it the 18th of June. From thence we continued our course to Sierra Leona, on the coast of Guinea, where we arrived the 22nd of July, and found necessary provisions, great store of elephants, oysters upon trees of one kind, spawning and increasing infinitely, the oyster suffering no bud to grow. We departed thence the four and twentieth day.

We arrived in England the third of November, 1580, being the third year of our departure.

Name _____

Voyage of Sir Francis Drake Cumulative Reading

Directions: Read aloud your assigned part with the group.

R1:   The famous voyage of Sir Francis Drake into the South Sea,

R1, R2:   and therehence about the whole Globe of the Earth,

R1, R2, R3:   begun in the year of our Lord 1577.

R2:   The 15th day of November, in the year of our Lord 1577,

R2, R3:   Master Francis Drake, with a fleet of five ships and barks,

R1, R2, R3:   and to the number of 164 men,

R3:   gentlemen and sailors,

R1, R3:   departed from Plymouth,

R1, R2, R3:   giving out his pretended voyage for Alexandria.

R1:   But the wind falling contrary,

R1, R2:   he was forced the next morning to put into Falmouth Haven, in Cornwall,

R1, R2, R3:   where such and so terrible a tempest took us,

R2:   as few men have seen the like, and was indeed so vehement that all our ships were like to have gone to wrack.

R2, R3:   But it pleased God to preserve us from that extremity and to afflict us only for that present with these two particulars:

R1, R2, R3:   the mast of our Admiral, which was the *Pelican*, was cut overboard for the safeguard of the ship,

R3:   and the *Marigold* was driven ashore, and somewhat bruised.

Voyage of Sir Francis Drake
Cumulative Reading (cont.)

R1, R3: For the repairing of which damages we returned again to Plymouth; and having recovered those harms, and brought the ships again to good state,

R1, R2, R3: we set forth the second time from Plymouth, and set sail the 13th day of December following.

R1: Not long before our departure, they told us that not far off there were such great ships as ours, wishing us to beware;

R1, R2: upon this our captain would stay no longer.

R1, R2, R3: From Java Major we sailed for the Cape of Good Hope, which was the first land we fell withal;

R2: neither did we touch with it, or any other land, until we came to Sierra Leona,

R2, R3: upon the coast of Guinea; notwithstanding we ran hard aboard the cape,

R1, R2, R3: finding the report of the Portugals to be most false who affirm that it is the most dangerous cape of the world,

R3: never without intolerable storms and present danger to travellers which come near the same.

R1, R3: This cape is a most stately thing, and the fairest cape we saw in the whole circumference of the earth,

R1, R2, R3: and we passed by it the 18th of June. From thence we continued our course to Sierra Leona, on the coast of Guinea,

R1: where we arrived the 22nd of July, and found necessary provisions, great store of elephants, oysters upon trees of one kind, spawning and increasing infinitely,

R1, R2: the oyster suffering no bud to grow. We departed thence the four and twentieth day.

R1, R2, R3: We arrived in England the third of November, 1580, being the third year of our departure.

Iroquois Poetry

Objective

√ Students will deliver oral presentations and read passages fluently with practice using recorded materials.

Materials

- copies of the poem "Magic Formula" (page 25) for the students
- copies of *Fluency Evaluation* (page 26) for the students
- copies of *Analyzing "Magic Formula"* (page 27) for the students
- video recorder and tape recorder with microphone

Fluency Suggestions and Activities

You may want to complete the history and/or vocabulary activities on the following page before this fluency activity. An understanding of the historical context and vocabulary will help students analyze and read the piece fluently.

1. Read the poem, "Magic Formula" (page 25), aloud to demonstrate fluency. Draw students' attention to your reading rate, voice tone, and expression.

2. Ask the students to discuss the meaning of the poem, and then ask them the following questions: What mood do you sense from this poem? How do you think the author's voice would sound when reading this? What kind of voice tone do you think should be used for reciting this poem? What kind of expression should be used? How could hand gestures be used to emphasize the meaning of the poem?

3. Explain to the students that they will have the chance to practice reading the poem by recording their voices and then evaluating their own fluency. Ask them how they think listening to their voice recordings might assist them with improving their fluency. Explain that by listening to their recorded readings of the poem, they will be able to listen to their accuracy, expression, and voice tone in order to make necessary changes.

4. Distribute student copies of the poem (page 25) and allow time in class for the students to practice reading. After practicing, provide each student the opportunity to record his or her reading of the poem. After recording, each student listens to the recording through headphones while following along with the passage. Encourage each student to pay attention to his or her reading rate, accuracy, smoothness of reading, and expression.

5. Then have the student complete the *Fluency Evaluation* (page 26) activity sheet to assess his or her progress. To complete this page, the student assesses his or her reading smoothness and rate of reading. The student will also record mispronounced words and assess his or her use of expression. Finally, the student creates a plan for improving fluency.

6. After reviewing the recording, each student records the passage again to try to make improvements. Encourage students to use hand motions and facial expressions as they read. Remind them of the mood being expressed in the poem and encourage them to reflect this mood in their readings. Finally, videotape students reading their poems and present them to the class and at an upcoming school event, such as parent night, conferences, or open house. You might want to complete this activity during American Indian Heritage month, which is celebrated in November each year.

Iroquois Poetry (cont.)

History Connection

Begin the lesson by introducing the poem "Magic Formula" and explaining the history of the Iroquois Indians using the information below.

Around 1600, five Iroquois tribes in the New York region, the Mohawks, the Oneidas, the Onondagas, the Cayugas, and the Senecas, joined together to form a confederacy. Every year, usually in the late summer or fall, each tribe sent a delegation of chiefs to the great council. Fifty chiefs would meet together. All decisions were reached after lengthy deliberation by the chiefs, and decisions were made by consensus. Each tribe had one vote equal to each of the others. Some of the most important democratic ideals used to form the country's government were learned from this confederation.

Vocabulary Connection

Discuss unfamiliar vocabulary encountered in the text. Some possible words are listed below. After identifying the difficult words, discuss them within the context of the text.

- **formula**—a set of rules for doing something
- **trouble**—worry
- **depart**—leave
- **devour**—swallow
- **mighty**—powerful or strong
- **subdue**—calm down

Extension Ideas

- Encourage analysis of the poem "Magic Formula" by having students meet in small groups to address and answer questions using the activity sheet, *Analyzing "Magic Formula"* (page 27).
- Allow students the opportunity to conduct further research about the Iroquois tribes or other American Indian tribes of interest. Encourage students to write short poems to reflect information they gathered from their research. Have them practice reading their poems and then perform them for the class.

Magic Formula

By the Iroquois Indians

Magic Formula

You have no right to trouble me,

Depart, I am becoming stronger.

You are now departing from me,

You who would devour me;

I am becoming stronger, stronger.

Mighty medicine is now within me,

You cannot now subdue me—

I am becoming stronger,

I am stronger, stronger, stronger.

Fluency Evaluation

Directions: Practice reading the poem, "Magic Formula." Ask for help with reading any words that are unfamiliar to you. Record your voice as you read the passage. Listen to the recording and complete this page to evaluate your reading fluency.

Name: _____

My reading was: very smooth   somewhat smooth   choppy

My reading rate was: too slow   just right   too fast

I made mistakes reading these words: _____

Did I use expression?   Yes   No

Here is my plan for improvement: _____

_____

_____

Directions: Practice reading the passage and record yourself again. Then, complete the evaluation again. Compare your two recordings.

My reading was: very smooth   somewhat smooth   choppy

My reading rate was: too slow   just right   too fast

I made mistakes reading these words: _____

Did I use expression?   Yes   No

Here is how my reading fluency changed: _____

_____

Name _____

Analyzing "Magic Formula"

Directions: Answer the questions below after discussing them with classmates.

1. What mood do you sense from the author?

_____

_____

_____

2. What words reflect this mood?

_____

_____

_____

3. Who or what do you think is the one "who would devour me"?

_____

_____

_____

4. What do you think is the "mighty medicine"?

_____

_____

5. How do you think the author is becoming stronger?

_____

_____

_____

6. What do you think inspired the author to write this poem?

_____

_____

_____

Pueblo Traditional Song

Objective

√ Students will deliver paired-reading, oral presentations, performing a poem for two voices fluently with changes in tone, voice, timing, and expression.

Materials

- overhead transparency of the song "Song of the Sky Loom" (page 30)
- copies of *"Song of the Sky Loom"—A Poem for Two Voices* (page 31) for the students
- copies of *Analyzing the "Song of the Sky Loom"* (page 32) for the students

Fluency Suggestions and Activities

You may want to complete the history and/or vocabulary activities on the following page before this fluency activity. An understanding of the historical context and vocabulary will help students analyze and read the piece fluently.

1. Read the song, "Song of the Sky Loom" (page 30), aloud for the students, modeling fluent reading, and ask them to offer their thoughts about what the poem means.

2. Explain to the students that they will all have the opportunity to perform this poem in pairs. (Arrange to have each pair of students present its poem for a different class or audience within the school. You could put a sign-up sheet in the teachers' lounge and ask for teachers who are willing to have your students visit their classrooms.)

3. Distribute copies of *"Song of the Sky Loom"—A Poem for Two Voices* (page 31) and draw students' attention to the layout of the words of the song. Explain that the song is divided into parts for Voice 1 and Voice 2. Voice 1 begins the reading because the first line of the poem is below that heading. The next line is under the heading Voice 2. Some lines of the poem are read together. These lines are bolded.

4. Encourage students to focus on voice tone, timing, and facial expressions as they read. Discuss with students how their tone of voice can affect the mood of the song. Discuss how the speed at which they read is important, as well. Emphasize to the students that since they are performing this reading, that it is important to think about their facial expressions because people will be watching them perform.

5. Invite two students to model reading a few lines of the song for the class. Tell the students that this kind of poem takes practice to read fluently. Divide the students into pairs and tell them that they will be performing this piece for another class in the school.

6. Allow the students time to practice reading their parts. You may want to have this practice time be spread out among several days. If you allow the students about 5–10 minutes each day and ask them to practice at home, as well, you will see marked improvement in their fluency with the song.

7. On the day of the presentations, allow students some practice time in your classroom before they give their presentations. You might want to complete this activity during American Indian Heritage month, which is celebrated in November each year.

Pueblo Traditional Song (cont.)

History Connection

Discuss the history of the song "Song of the Sky Loom" using the information below.

The Tewa Pueblo tribe are a group of southwestern Indians who live north of Santa Fe, New Mexico. The "Song of the Sky Loom" is about a light rain in the desert. Rain is extremely important to life in the high desert environment. The fact that desert wildlife can survive without water for long periods of time makes the desert rains that much more spectacular. This particular ritual song to nature shows the use of repetition in early American literature. The storytellers of the American Indian tribes, like the Tewa, used repetition to help them more easily remember their songs and tales.

Vocabulary Connection

Discuss unfamiliar vocabulary encountered in the text. Some possible words are listed below. After identifying the difficult words, discuss them within the context of the text.

- **garment**—piece of clothing
- **brightness**—colorful and light
- **warp**—a knitted fabric with the pattern running lengthwise
- **weft**—a knitted fabric with the pattern running crosswise or in a circular direction
- **fringes**—the edge decoration
- **border**—the edge
- **fittingly**—suitably

Extension Ideas

- Have students work with their partners to analyze the song using the activity sheet, *Analyzing the "Song of the Sky Loom"* (page 32). Encourage them to refer back to the song as they discuss it and answer the questions. You might offer this analysis sheet to the teachers who are having your students present. They might like to use it with their students as a way to ensure that the students listen to the presentation.

- Have the class perform the song for two voices in a different way. Divide the class in half. Students in one half are assigned to Voice 1, and students in the other half are assigned to Voice 2. Have them perform a class reading of the song for parents or at a school assembly.

Song of the Sky Loom

A Tewa Pueblo Traditional Poem

O our Mother the Earth, O our Father the Sky,

Your children are we, and with tired backs

We bring you the gifts you love.

Then weave for us a garment of brightness;

May the warp be the white light of morning,

May the weft be the red light of evening,

May the fringes be the falling rain,

May the border be the standing rainbow.

Thus weave for us a garment of brightness

That we may walk fittingly where birds sing,

That we may walk fittingly where grass is green,

O our Mother the Earth, O our Father the Sky!

The "sky loom" refers to a desert rain where the rain showers hang lightly from the sky.

Names _____

"Song of the Sky Loom"— A Poem for Two Voices

Voice 1

O our Mother the Earth,

Your children are we,

We bring you the gifts you love.

Then weave for us a garment

May the warp be

of morning,

May the weft be the red light of evening,

May the border be the standing rainbow.

That we may walk

where birds sing,

fittingly

O our Mother the Earth,

O our Father the Sky!

Voice 2

O our Father the Sky,

and with tired backs

We bring you the gifts you love.

of brightness;

the white light

of morning,

May the fringes be the falling rain,

Thus weave for us a garment of brightness

fittingly

That we may walk

where grass is green,

O our Mother the Earth,

O our Father the Sky!

Name _____

Analyzing the "Song of the Sky Loom"

Directions: Answer the following questions with your partner.

1. Why do the Pueblo people refer to "Mother Earth" and "Father Sky"?

   _____

   _____

2. Why do they feel like "children" of the earth and sky?

   _____

   _____

3. What gifts do you think the people bring?

   _____

   _____

4. What things do you think are important to the Pueblos?

   _____

   _____

   _____

5. Do you think the Pueblos were gentle or aggressive people? Explain.

   _____

   _____

   _____

   _____

   _____

Learning about Pilgrims

Objective

√ Students will read passages fluently and accurately within an oral paired-reading activity, focusing on correct phrasing.

Materials

- copies of the poem "The Little Pilgrim" (page 35) for the students
- copies of *Analyzing "The Little Pilgrim"* (page 36) for the students
- video recorder and videotape

Fluency Suggestions and Activities

You may want to complete the history and/or vocabulary activities on the following page before this fluency activity. An understanding of the historical context and vocabulary will help students analyze and read the piece fluently.

1. Explain to the students, that when reading poetry, it is necessary to use proper phrasing. Define *phrasing* as grouping together groups of words.

2. Demonstrate reading that does not utilize correct phrasing, by reading the first stanza of "The Little Pilgrim" below. Be sure to pause at each slash mark (/) between words. Draw students' attention to the fact that the stanza is difficult to understand when read in this manner.

   There is a / path that leads / to God All others / go astray—
   Narrow, but / pleasant is the / road, And / Christians love / the way.

3. Next, read the stanza again, pausing only at the end of each line, as follows:

   There is a path that leads to God (pause) All others go astray (pause) Narrow, but pleasant is the road, (pause) And Christians love the way.

4. Ask the students to explain the difference between the two readings of the stanza. They will likely say that the second reading was smooth and made more sense. Explain that the second reading used correct phrasing. The words were chunked together in a more meaningful way. Point out to students that reading word-by-word also makes phrasing difficult to accomplish. Read the stanza again in a choppy, word-by-word manner. This kind of reading is difficult to understand and not as pleasant to hear.

5. Provide each student with a copy of the "The Little Pilgrim" (page 35). Ask the students to read silently as you read the first two stanzas of the poems. Instruct them to take notice of the way the words are read fluidly with pauses at the ends of the lines. Explain that pauses also take place briefly when commas are inserted in the lines of the poem. Then instruct them to read a few stanzas along with you to practice oral reading with attention to phrasing. Next, allow the students time to practice reading the poem independently.

6. Then divide them into pairs to read the poem aloud. You might want to suggest that the partners take turns reading alternating stanzas of the poem. Encourage the students to vary the tone in their voices and to read with expression to enhance the meaning of the poem.

7. When students have had the opportunity to practice reading the poem several times and on a few different occasions, ask them to recite the poem to classmates in small groups of three or four students. Make a video of the students' presentations and send the tape to Plimoth Plantation in Plymouth, Massachusetts.

Learning about Pilgrims (cont.)

History Connection

Discuss the history of why the Pilgrims came to America using the information below.

The Pilgrims wanted to leave the Church of England because they didn't agree with all of the Church's beliefs. They separated and started a new church. The Pilgrims were afraid that they would be arrested in England, so they traveled north across the sea. They settled in Holland (The Netherlands) where people had the freedom to choose how they worship. The Pilgrims missed living in England. They wanted their children to grow up with British ideas, not Dutch ideas. After 10 years, the Pilgrims planned to move again. This time, they decided to cross the Atlantic Ocean and settle in America. In a new colony they could live like Britishmen, but most important, they would be free to worship in their own way.

Vocabulary Connection

Discuss unfamiliar vocabulary encountered in the text. Some possible words are listed below. After identifying the difficult words, discuss them within the context of the text.

- **astray**—off the right path
- **strait**—straight
- **thro'**—through
- **tread**—walk
- **snare**—trap
- **sinners**—people who have done something bad
- **feeble**—weak
- **condescend**—to look down on someone
- **venture**—carry on even when it is dangerous

Extension Ideas

- Assist the students in their understanding of the poem by asking them questions about it. Distribute copies of the activity sheet, *Analyzing "The Little Pilgrim"* (page 36). Then group the students in threes or fours to discuss and answer the questions.
- Divide students into groups of three or four. Have the students think about how the poem could be reenacted as a pantomime. Encourage them to discuss the actions that could be dramatized in each of the stanzas. To perform the dramatization, one or two students read the poem as the other two perform the actions.

The Little Pilgrim

Printed in Massachusetts

There is a path that leads to God—
All others go astray—
Narrow, but pleasant is the road,
And Christians love the way.

It leads strait thro' this world of sin;
And dangers must be pass'd;
But those who boldly walk therein;
Will come to heaven at last.

How shall an infant Pilgrim dare
This dangerous path to tread?
For on the way is many a snare
For youthful travellers spread.

While the broad road that thousands go,
Lies near, and opens fair:
And many turn aside I know,
To walk with sinners there.

But, lest my feeble steps should slide,
Or wander from thy way,
Lord, condescend to be my guide,
And I shall never stray.

Then I may go without alarm,
And trust his word of old;
The lambs he'll gather with his arm,
And lead them to his fold.

Thus I may safely venture through,
Beneath my shepherd's care;
And keep the gate of heaven in view,
Till I shall enter there.

Source: The Library of Congress

Name _____

Analyzing "The Little Pilgrim"

Directions: Reread "The Little Pilgrim." Work with your group to answer the questions below.

1. What does the poem say about the path that leads to God?

   _____

   _____

2. What is dangerous about the path?

   _____

   _____

3. What do you think the word *condescend* means?

   _____

   _____

4. Look up the definition of the word *condescend* in the dictionary and record it below.

   _____

   _____

5. Read the stanza containing the word *condescend*. What does it mean when used in this way?

   _____

   _____

6. What message do you think the author is trying to communicate through this poem?

   _____

   _____

   _____

   _____

   _____

   _____

Slavery in America

Objective

√ Students will use repeated reading as a method of improving reading fluency.

Materials

- copies of the poem "The Slave's Dream" (page 39) for the students
- one copy of *Repeated Reading Tips* (page 40)
- copies of *Peer Fluency Evaluation* (page 41) for the students

Fluency Suggestions and Activities

You may want to complete the history and/or vocabulary activities on the following page before this fluency activity. An understanding of the historical context and vocabulary will help students analyze and read the piece fluently.

1. Explain to students that reading fluently takes practice. When reading a text for the first time, it isn't easy to read smoothly and with expression. This kind of reading develops over time and is enhanced with repeated readings of the same text. You might want to demonstrate this by reading a passage of text out of an encyclopedia or a complex science textbook. Show the students how, with repeated attempts, your reading becomes smoother and more rapid.

2. Introduce the poem, "The Slave's Dream" (page 39), and ask the students to tell what they think it will be about. Give each student a copy of the "The Slave's Dream" (page 39). Explain that their task will be to read the poem several times to increase fluency.

3. Read over the page, *Repeated Reading Tips* (page 40) with students, and post it for future reference.

4. Allow each student to practice reading the poem independently.

5. Then, pair students for continued practice. Instruct students to set common goals and work together to read with fluency. Provide each student with a *Peer Fluency Evaluation* (page 41). To use the form, one child reads the passage three times while the partner listens. After the second and third readings, the partner completes the form.

6. Encourage the partners to discuss the reading after each time, offering encouragement and suggestions. To assist with discussion, post the following statements in a location where students can refer to them, if necessary.

   Encouraging Statements: You used great expression. I like how smoothly you read. Your phrasing was great. Your voice had good tone when you read.

   Suggestion Statements: That was good, but try not to read choppily next time. Good job, but next time try reading with more expression. Take your time because you were a little bit too fast.

Slavery in America (cont.)

History Connection

Discuss the history of slavery using the information below as well as further information on slavery.

In the early 1600s, the first Africans were brought over to America as indentured servants. Soon after, the Atlantic slave trade began. Slave trade was a very profitable business. British and colonial ships traveled to Africa. There, traders picked up human captives. They were put on the ships and taken to the colonies. Once the ships reached the colonies, the traders sold their captives.

This poem by Henry Wadsworth Longfellow was published in 1842 as part of a collection called *Poems of Slavery*.

Vocabulary Connection

Discuss unfamiliar vocabulary encountered in the text. Some possible words are listed below. After identifying the difficult words, discuss them within the context of the text.

- **sickle**—a tool used by farmers to cut their crop
- **Niger**—a river in Africa
- **scabbard**—a case or cover for a sword
- **smiting**—hitting
- **flank**—the area on an animal between its ribs and hip
- **tamarind**—a type of tree
- **myriad**—a large number of
- **tempestuous**—loud and excited
- **illumined**—lit up
- **fetter**—chains that hold someone a prisoner

Extension Idea

- Divide the poem into sections of two to four lines. Assign a section of the poem to each pair of students. Have the students practice reading together their assigned part. Then gather the class together for a group reading of the poem, with each pair of students reading its part of the poem at the appropriate time.

The Slave's Dream

By Henry Wadsworth Longfellow

Beside the ungathered rice he lay,
　　His sickle in his hand;
His breast was bare, his matted hair
　　Was buried in the sand.
Again, in the mist and shadow of sleep,
　　He saw his Native Land.

Wide through the landscape of his dreams
　　The lordly Niger flowed;
Beneath the palm-trees on the plain
　　Once more a king he strode;
And heard the tinkling caravans
　　Descend the mountain-road.

He saw once more his dark-eyed queen
　　Among her children stand;
They clasped his neck, they kissed his cheeks,
　　They held him by the hand!—
A tear burst from the sleeper's lids
　　And fell into the sand.

And then at furious speed he rode
　　Along the Niger's bank;
His bridle-reins were golden chains,
　　And, with a martial clank,
At each leap he could feel his scabbard of steel
　　Smiting his stallion's flank.

Before him, like a blood-red flag,
　　The bright flamingoes flew;
From morn till night he followed their flight,
　　O'er plains where the tamarind grew,
Till he saw the roofs of Caffre huts,
　　And the ocean rose to view.

At night he heard the lion roar,
　　And the hyena scream,
And the river-horse, as he crushed the reeds
　　Beside some hidden stream;
And it passed, like a glorious roll of drums,
　　Through the triumph of his dream.

The forests, with their myriad tongues,
　　Shouted of liberty;
And the Blast of the Desert cried aloud,
　　With a voice so wild and free,
That he started in his sleep and smiled
　　At their tempestuous glee.

He did not feel the driver's whip,
　　Nor the burning heat of day;
For Death had illumined the Land of Sleep,
　　And his lifeless body lay
A worn-out fetter, that the soul
　　Had broken and thrown away!

Repeated Reading Tips

- Read through the passage silently from beginning to end.

- Ask for assistance pronouncing difficult or unfamiliar words.

- Select one part of the text to read. Read it aloud several times.

- Be sure to use expression when you read.

- Pause in appropriate places.

- Practice each section of the passage in the same manner.

- Finally, read the passage from beginning to end.

- Now, read the passage to someone else.

Name _____

Peer Fluency Evaluation

Directions: Select a partner. Choose a passage to read aloud to your partner. Read the passage aloud three times. Have your partner complete the chart below after your second and third readings.

	Second Reading	**Third Reading**
Improved Accuracy		
Read Faster		
Read Smoother		
Read with Better Expression		

1. Have your partner write two compliments about your reading fluency.

_____

_____

_____

_____

2. Have your partner write one suggestion for practice.

_____

_____

_____

The Boston Tea Party

Objective

√ Students will identify and evaluate elements of fluency as they listen to oral reading of text.

Materials

- copies of the short essay "Recollections of the Boston Tea Party" (page 44) for the students
- copies of *Elements of Fluency* (page 45) for the students
- copies of *Oral Reading Fluency Evaluation* (page 46) for the students

Fluency Suggestions and Activities

You may want to complete the history and/or vocabulary activities on the following page before this fluency activity. An understanding of the historical context and vocabulary will help students analyze and read the piece fluently.

1. Explain to the students that there are many things to consider when learning to read with fluency-rate of reading, loudness, accuracy, and expression. Review each of the elements with the students.

   Rate of Reading: This refers to the speed of reading. It is important to read with a proper speed. If reading is too slow or too fast, it is distracting and difficult to understand.

   Loudness: This refers to how loud or soft a person reads. If reading is too soft, it is difficult to hear. If it is too loud, it can be distracting. Loudness varies depending on the size of the audience. A reader uses a softer voice with a small group and a louder voice with a large group of listeners.

   Accuracy: This refers to the correctness of reading. Reading with accuracy means reading without errors.

   Smoothness: Reading that is choppy is difficult to understand. Smoothness refers to reading that is smooth and has appropriate pauses.

   Expression: This refers to the reader's ability to add expression to his or her reading. The reading should communicate the mood of the text. If the text communicates an enthusiastic message, the expression should match this mood.

2. Explain to the students that they will have the chance to evaluate the elements of fluency as you read "Recollections of the Boston Tea Party" (page 44). Provide each student with copies of the activity sheets, *Elements of Fluency* (page 45) and *Oral Reading Fluency Evaluation* (page 46). Review the pages. Explain that the fluency page contains information explaining what to listen for during the reading. The evaluation page is for recording their impressions of your fluency as you read the selection.

3. Read the first paragraph of the selection and then discuss the elements of fluency. Read the text aloud from beginning to end. As you read, the students should listen and evaluate your fluency and record their responses on the evaluation sheets.

4. After the reading, divide students into small groups and have them discuss their evaluations and suggestions.

The Boston Tea Party (cont.)

History Connection

Review the history of the Boston Tea Party using the information provided below.

When Parliament repealed the Townshend Acts, they decided to keep the tax on tea. This was to show the colonists that Great Britain still had the power to tax its citizens. The colonists knew exactly what their leaders were up to, and they did not like it. Some colonists refused to buy British tea for more than five years.

Then, Parliament passed something called the Tea Act. This law allowed only some shop owners to import and sell tea. The colonists did not want Britain having so much control over their economy. A Boston man named Samuel Adams gave many speeches. He excited people and made them angry at Great Britain's leaders. He was a member of the Sons of Liberty. These men protested in the streets. One night in December 1773, some men dressed up as Indians and went aboard ships in Boston Harbor. They broke open 342 chests of tea and dumped it all into the harbor. The people cheered this "Boston Tea Party."

Vocabulary Connection

Discuss unfamiliar vocabulary encountered in the text. Some possible words are listed below. After identifying the difficult words, discuss them within the context of the text.

- **associates**—people who you work with or who are your partners
- **denominated**—named
- **tomahawk**—an axe used by American Indians
- **blacksmith**—a person who works with metal
- **wharf**—a structure in a harbor where ships pick up and drop off cargo
- **boatswain**—the sailor on a ship who looks after the hull
- **residence**—the place where people live
- **transaction**—an activity between two people or groups

Extension Idea

- Provide copies of "Recollections of the Boston Tea Party" (page 44) to students. Ask them to select portions of the text to practice reading. Then have them recite the text to classmates. Encourage classmates to use the *Elements of Fluency* (page 45) and *Oral Reading Fluency Evaluation* (page 46) to assess reading fluency.

Recollections of the Boston Tea Party

By George R. T. Hewes

I dressed myself in the costume of an Indian, equipped with a small hatchet, which I and my associates denominated the tomahawk, with which, and a club, after having painted my face and hands with coal dust in the shop of a blacksmith, I repaired to Griffin's wharf, where the ships lay that contained the tea. When I first appeared in the street after being thus disguised, I fell in with many who were dressed, equipped and painted as I was, and who fell in with me and marched in order to the place of our destination.

When we arrived at the wharf, there were three of our number who assumed an authority to direct our operations, to which we readily submitted. They divided us into three parties, for the purpose of boarding the three ships which contained the tea at the same time. The name of him who commanded the division to which I was assigned was Leonard Pitt. The names of the other commanders I never knew. We were immediately ordered by the respective commanders to board all the ships at the same time, which we promptly obeyed. The commander of the division to which I belonged, as soon as we were on board the ship, appointed me boatswain, and ordered me to go to the captain and demand of him the keys to the hatches and a dozen candles. I made the demand accordingly, and the captain promptly replied, and delivered the articles; but requested me at the same time to do no damage to the ship or rigging. We then were ordered by our commander to open the hatches and take out all the chests of tea and throw them overboard, and we immediately proceeded to execute his orders, first cutting and splitting the chests with our tomahawks, so as thoroughly to expose them to the effects of the water.

In about three hours from the time we went on board, we had thus broken and thrown overboard every tea chest to be found in the ship, while those in the other ships were disposing of the tea in the same way, at the same time. We were surrounded by British armed ships, but no attempt was made to resist us.

We then quietly retired to our several places of residence, without having any conversation with each other, or taking any measures to discover who were our associates; nor do I recollect of our having had the knowledge of the name of a single individual concerned in that affair, except that of Leonard Pitt, the commander of my division, whom I have mentioned. There appeared to be an understanding that each individual should volunteer his services, keep his own secret, and risk the consequence for himself. No disorder took place during that transaction, and it was observed at that time that the stillest night ensued that Boston had enjoyed for many months.

Name _____

Elements of Fluency

Rate of Reading

- How is the speed of reading?
- Is it too fast? Is it too slow?
- Is the speed of the reading easy to understand?
- Is the reading speed distracting?

Loudness

- Is the reading too soft?
- Is the reading too loud?
- Is it just right?
- Does the loudness of the reading match the size of the audience?

Accuracy

- Does the reader pronounce the words correctly?
- Does the reader skip words?

Smoothness

- Is the reading smooth?
- Is the reading choppy?
- Does the reader speed up and slow down?

Expression

- Does the reader use expression?
- Does the expression match the mood of the text?

Name _____

Oral Reading Fluency Evaluation

Directions: Listen to the reader. Circle your choices below. Write your comments at the bottom of the page.

Rate of Reading

Too fast   Too slow   Just right

Easy to understand   Difficult to understand

Loudness

Too loud   Too soft   Just right

Matches audience size   Doesn't match audience size

Accuracy

Correct pronunciation   Many mispronounced words

Skipped words   Didn't skip words

Smoothness

Smooth reading   Choppy reading

Reading that speeds up and slows down

Reading smoothness just right

Expression

Expression   No expression

Expression matches text   Expression doesn't match text

Additional comments: _____

_____

Liberty in the Colonies

Objective

√ Students will participate in a cooperative reading activity to enhance expressive reading skills by engaging in cumulative choral reading.

Materials

- copies of the poem "Liberty Tree" (page 49) for the students
- copies of *"Liberty Tree"—Cumulative Choral Reading* (pages 50–51) for the students
- copies of *Analyzing the "Liberty Tree"* (page 52) for the students

Fluency Suggestions and Activities

You may want to complete the history and/or vocabulary activities on the following page before this fluency activity. An understanding of the historical context and vocabulary will help students analyze and read the piece fluently.

1. Read the poem, "Liberty Tree" (page 49), by Thomas Paine aloud, modeling fluent reading.

2. Explain to the students that they will read "Liberty Tree" as a cumulative choral reading activity. This means that one student will read a line, then another student joins the first student, and then a third student joins in. Demonstrate this process with student volunteers using the passages below.

R1:	In a chariot of light
R1 and R2:	from the regions of day,
R1, R2, R3:	The Goddess of Liberty came;

3. Divide the students into groups of three and distribute copies of the *"Liberty Tree"—Cumulative Choral Reading* (pages 50–51). Assign each student in the group a part to read. Explain that R1, R2, and R3 stand for Reader 1, Reader 2, and Reader 3. Draw their attention to the way a new reader is added on each line—first one reader, then two, then three reading together at the same time.

4. Have the students discuss words or phrases that should carry particular expressive emphasis.

5. Allow students time in class to practice their cumulative readings of the text.

6. Have students present their versions of the reading to the class. Then arrange to have students perform their readings for the classes at their grade level or another grade level also studying the American Revolution. You could also arrange to have one of the groups read over the loud speaker during the school's morning announcements.

Liberty in the Colonies (cont.)

History Connection

Begin the lesson by introducing Thomas Paine and discussing the historical information provided below. Read the title of the text selection and ask them to discuss the concept of *liberty* by asking the following questions: What is another word for liberty? When have you heard the word *liberty* used before? What does liberty mean to you in your life today? How would your life be different without liberty?

Thomas Paine was a Patriot during the years leading up to the American Revolution. Not only did he believe that the colonists had a right to protest the actions of the British, but he believed the colonists should declare their independence from Great Britian. He is best known for writing *Common Sense* as propaganda to convince people to declare independence from Britain.

This poem describes how people had come to America because of the promise of liberty. These people had fought for Great Britain to defend the land. Now, Great Britain was threatening to take away their freedom. The poem calls for Americans to fight back.

Vocabulary Connection

Discuss unfamiliar vocabulary encountered in the text. Some possible words are listed below. After identifying the difficult words, discuss them within the context of the text.

- **chariot**—wheeled vehicle usually pulled by horses
- **celestials**—angels or other heavenly beings
- **hither**—here
- **exotic**—different and unknown
- **endued**—put on
- **unvexed**—not bothered by
- **groat**—old British coin
- **swains**—male admirers
- **profane**—not concerned with religion
- **amain**—to do something with all one's strength
- **flee**—to run away

Extension Idea

- To assist the students in increasing their understanding of the poem, have them work with their groups to complete the activity sheet, *Analyzing the "Liberty Tree"* (page 52). You may want to have them complete this page before their public performances in order to assist them with comprehension, which will help with their reading expression.

Liberty Tree

By Thomas Paine

In a chariot of light from the regions of day,
The Goddess of Liberty came;
Ten thousand celestials directed the way
And hither conducted the dame.
A fair budding branch from the gardens above,
Where millions with millions agree,
She brought in her hand as a pledge of her love,
And the plant she named Liberty Tree.

The celestial exotic struck deep in the ground,
Like a native it flourished and bore;
The fame of its fruit drew the nations around,
To seek out this peaceable shore.
Unmindful of names or distinction they came,
For freemen like brothers agree;
With one spirit endued, they one friendship pursued,
And their temple was Liberty Tree.

Beneath this fair tree, like the patriarchs of old,
Their bread in contentment they ate,
Unvexed with the troubles of silver and gold,
The cares of the grand and the great.

With timber and tar they Old England supplied,
And supported her power on the sea;
Her battles they fought, without getting a groat,
For the honor of Liberty Tree.

But hear, O ye swains, 'tis a tale most profane,
How all the tyrannical powers,
Kings, Commons, and Lords, are uniting amain
To cut down this guardian of ours;
From the east to the west blow the trumpet to arms
Through the land let the sound of it flee,
Let the far and the near, all unite with a cheer,
In defence of our Liberty Tree.

Name _____

"Liberty Tree"— Cumulative Choral Reading

R1:	In a chariot of light
R1 and R2:	from the regions of day,
R1, R2, R3:	The Goddess of Liberty came;
R2:	Ten thousand celestials
R2 and R3:	directed the way
R1, R2, R3:	And hither conducted the dame.
R3:	A fair budding branch
R3 and R1:	from the gardens above,
R1, R2, R3:	Where millions with millions agree,
R1:	She brought in her hand
R1 and R2:	as a pledge of her love,
R1, R2, R3:	And the plant she named Liberty Tree.
R2:	The celestial exotic
R2 and R3:	struck deep in the ground,
R1, R2, R3:	Like a native it flourished and bore;
R3:	The fame of its fruit
R3 and R1:	drew the nations around,
R1, R2, R3:	To seek out this peaceable shore.
R1:	Unmindful of names
R1 and R2:	or distinction they came,
R1, R2, R3:	For freemen like brothers agree;
R2:	With one spirit endued,
R2 and R3:	they one friendship pursued,
R1, R2, R3:	And their temple was Liberty Tree.

"Liberty Tree"—
Cumulative Choral Reading *(cont.)*

R3:	Beneath this fair tree,
R3 and R1:	like the patriarchs of old,
R1, R2, R3:	Their bread in contentment they ate,
R1:	Unvexed with the troubles
R1 and R2:	of silver and gold,
R1, R2, R3:	The cares of the grand and the great.
R2:	With timber and tar
R2 and R3:	they Old England supplied,
R1, R2, R3:	And supported her power on the sea;
R3:	Her battles they fought,
R3 and R1:	without getting a groat,
R1, R2, R3:	For the honor of Liberty Tree.
R1:	But hear, O ye swains,
R1 and R2:	'tis a tale most profane,
R1, R2, R3:	How all the tyrannical powers,
R2:	Kings, Commons, and Lords,
R2 and R3:	are uniting amain
R1, R2, R3:	To cut down this guardian of ours;
R3:	From the east to the west
R3 and R1:	blow the trumpet to arms
R1, R2, R3:	Through the land let the sound of it flee,
R1:	Let the far and the near,
R1 and R2:	all unite with a cheer,
R1, R2, R3:	In defence of our Liberty Tree.

Name _____

Analyzing the "Liberty Tree"

Directions: Work with your group to answer the questions below.

1. Who do you think is the "Goddess of Liberty"?

   _____

   _____

2. What are celestials?

   _____

   _____

3. What was the pledge of the goddess' love?

   _____

   _____

4. What did the people do at the Liberty Tree?

   _____

   _____

5. Why do you think people want to cut down the tree?

   _____

   _____

6. List three unfamiliar phrases and determine their meanings.

           Phrases   Meanings

   _____   _____

   _____   _____

   _____   _____

7. What do you think is the general message of this poem?

   _____

   _____

   _____

   _____

   _____

Declaring Independence

Objective

√ Students will determine the meaning of text and then participate in an oral reading and explanation of it for other students.

Materials

- copies of *Excerpt from the Declaration of Independence* (page 55) for the students
- copies of *The Declaration of Independence Rewritten* (page 56) for the students
- copies of *Fluency Assessment* (page 57) for the students
- copies of *Analyzing the Declaration of Independence* (page 58) for the students
- pencils or highlighters
- tape recorder with microphone

Fluency Suggestions and Activities

You may want to complete the history and/or vocabulary activities on the following page before this fluency activity. An understanding of the historical context and vocabulary will help students analyze and read the piece fluently.

1. Read aloud the excerpt from the Declaration of Independence (page 55). Explain that it is not surprising that it might be difficult to understand it because people speak differently today than they did in the days this text was written.

2. Then read the rewritten version (page 56).

3. Give student pairs copies of both (pages 55–56) and have them compare the two versions and discuss their understanding of the text.

4. Explain that for this oral reading presentation, they will be asked to practice reading a rewritten version of the excerpt of the Declaration of Independence. Draw their attention to *The Declaration of Independence Rewritten* (page 56). Give copies of this page to any students who do not have one. Explain that as they read, they will focus on the use of expression. Have the students underline or highlight words, phrases, or sentences that should be emphasized when reading.

5. Provide students time in class to practice reading the text, focusing on accuracy, tone, and expression. Allow them to tape record their readings and then play back the recordings listening for the essentials of fluency. Provide copies of the *Fluency Assessment* (page 57) for the students to use as they evaluate their fluency.

6. Arrange a public reading of historical texts for other students in the school. For this reading, your students can select this or any other primary source already introduced in class. Students may present their oral readings independently or in small groups, depending on the format of the readings (reader's theater, poem for two voices, etc.).

Declaring Independence (cont.)

History Connection

Begin the lesson by reviewing the history of the Declaration of Independence. Ask the students if they know when and why it was written. On pages 59–60 is *The Complete Text of the Declaration of Independence* if you would like to have students read more of this document.

In 1776, the colonists sent delegates to Philadelphia for the Second Continental Congress. At first, most of the delegates thought that the colonists should remain British citizens. Then, the delegates began to think that liberty was their only choice. In June 1776, a delegate named Richard Henry Lee got up to speak. He proposed that Congress finally declare independence from Great Britain.

Congress chose a committee of five men to write the declaration. This committee decided it would be too hard to write as a group. Instead they decided to have one person, Thomas Jefferson, write the essay. The group told Jefferson three things he had to write about. He had to describe what makes a good government. Then, he had to explain why King George III had not done a good job. Finally, he had to announce that the colonists were declaring themselves free of Great Britain.

Vocabulary Connection

Discuss unfamiliar vocabulary encountered in the text. Some possible words are listed below. After identifying the difficult words, discuss them within the context of the text.

- **endowed**—provided
- **unalienable**—something that cannot be taken away
- **instituted**—set up
- **deriving**—getting
- **prudence**—using reason to govern and discipline
- **transient**—something that passes quickly
- **hath shewn**—has shown
- **usurpations**—things that were taken through force
- **despotism**—to be ruled by one person
- **tyranny**—complete control and power

Extension Idea

- Divide students into small groups to complete the activity sheet, *Analyzing the Declaration of Independence* (page 58). Allow the students time for discussion and research to assist with their responses.

Excerpt from the Declaration of Independence

WE hold these Truths to be self-evident, that all Men are created equal, that they are endowed by their Creator with certain unalienable Rights, that among these are Life, Liberty and the Pursuit of Happiness—That to secure these Rights, Governments are instituted among Men, deriving their just Powers from the Consent of the Governed, that whenever any Form of Government becomes destructive of these Ends, it is the Right of the People to alter or to abolish it, and to institute new Government, laying its Foundation on such Principles, and organizing its Powers in such Form, as to them shall seem most likely to effect their Safety and Happiness. Prudence, indeed, will dictate that Governments long established should not be changed for light and transient Causes; and accordingly all Experience hath shewn, that Mankind are more disposed to suffer, while Evils are sufferable, than to right themselves by abolishing the Forms to which they are accustomed. But when a long Train of Abuses and Usurpations, pursuing invariably the same Object, evinces a Design to reduce them under absolute Despotism, it is their Right, it is their Duty, to throw off such Government, and to provide new Guards for their future Security. Such has been the patient Sufferance of these Colonies; and such is now the Necessity which constrains them to alter their former Systems of Government. The History of the present King of Great-Britain is a History of repeated Injuries and Usurpations, all having in direct Object the Establishment of an absolute Tyranny over these States. To prove this, let Facts be submitted to a candid World.

Name_____

Excerpt from the Declaration of Independence Rewritten

We believe that all men are created equal. They are given by their Creator certain rights. Among these are Life, Liberty and the Pursuit of Happiness. To protect these rights, governments are set up among men, gaining their powers from the approval of the people. Whenever any form of government becomes harmful to these goals, it is the right of the people to change or to do away with it. It is their right to set up new government based on their beliefs and organized in favor of their safety and happiness. Good sense, indeed, will order that governments should not be changed for temporary causes. All experience has shown that people are more likely to suffer, while evils are tolerated. They would rather suffer than get rid of the things that are familiar to them. But when a long history of cruelty holds them down, it is their right, it is their duty, to get rid of this government, and to provide new guards for their future security. This has been the case for the colonies; and it is necessary for them to change their former systems of government. The history of the present king of Great Britain is a history of repeated injuries and attacks, all having the goal of absolute control over these states. To prove this, let facts be submitted to a uncomplicated world.

Name_____

Fluency Assessment

Directions: Listen to the recording of your voice. Answer the following questions.

1. What do you like about the way you read?

   _____

   _____

2. What don't you like about the way you read?

   _____

   _____

3. Was the reading too fast, too slow, or just right?

   _____

   _____

4. Did you stumble on any words? Explain.

   _____

   _____

5. Which words or phrases did you emphasize in the reading and why did you choose to emphasize them?

   _____

   _____

   _____

   _____

6. Practice reading the text again. Then make another recording. On the lines below, write your plan for improving your fluency for the next recording.

   _____

   _____

   _____

   _____

   _____

Name_____

Analyzing the Declaration of Independence

Directions: Meet with your classmates to answer the questions below. You will need to conduct research in order to answer some of the questions.

1. Why is it important to emphasize that "all men are created equal"? Why does it not say "men and women"?

   _____

   _____

   _____

2. Why is it necessary to have a government? What could happen without one?

   _____

   _____

   _____

3. What does the following statement mean? "All Experience has shown, that people are more likely to suffer, while Evils are tolerated. They would rather suffer than get rid of the things that are familiar to them."

   _____

   _____

   _____

4. Think about the government in our country. Does it have absolute control? In what areas does the government not control our lives?

   _____

   _____

   _____

   _____

   _____

The Complete Text of the Declaration of Independence

Action of Second Continental Congress, July 4, 1776

The unanimous Declaration of the thirteen United States of America

WHEN in the Course of human Events, it becomes necessary for one People to dissolve the Political Bands which have connected them with another, and to assume among the Powers of the Earth, the separate and equal Station to which the Laws of Nature and of Nature's God entitle them, a decent Respect to the Opinions of Mankind requires that they should declare the causes which impel them to the Separation.

WE hold these Truths to be self-evident, that all Men are created equal, that they are endowed by their Creator with certain unalienable Rights, that among these are Life, Liberty and the Pursuit of Happiness—That to secure these Rights, Governments are instituted among Men, deriving their just Powers from the Consent of the Governed, that whenever any Form of Government becomes destructive of these Ends, it is the Right of the People to alter or to abolish it, and to institute new Government, laying its Foundation on such Principles, and organizing its Powers in such Form, as to them shall seem most likely to effect their Safety and Happiness. Prudence, indeed, will dictate that Governments long established should not be changed for light and transient Causes; and accordingly all Experience hath shewn, that Mankind are more disposed to suffer, while Evils are sufferable, than to right themselves by abolishing the Forms to which they are accustomed. But when a long Train of Abuses and Usurpations, pursuing invariably the same Object, evinces a Design to reduce them under absolute Despotism, it is their Right, it is their Duty, to throw off such Government, and to provide new Guards for their future Security. Such has been the patient Sufferance of these Colonies; and such is now the Necessity which constrains them to alter their former Systems of Government. The History of the present King of Great- Britain is a History of repeated Injuries and Usurpations, all having in direct Object the Establishment of an absolute Tyranny over these States. To prove this, let Facts be submitted to a candid World.

HE has refused his Assent to Laws, the most wholesome and necessary for the public Good.

HE has forbidden his Governors to pass Laws of immediate and pressing Importance, unless suspended in their Operation till his Assent should be obtained; and when so suspended, he has utterly neglected to attend to them.

HE has refused to pass other Laws for the Accommodation of large Districts of People, unless those People would relinquish the Right of Representation in the Legislature, a Right inestimable to them, and formidable to Tyrants only.

HE has called together Legislative Bodies at Places unusual, uncomfortable, and distant from the Depository of their public Records, for the sole Purpose of fatiguing them into Compliance with his Measures.

HE has dissolved Representative Houses repeatedly, for opposing with manly Firmness his Invasions on the Rights of the People.

HE has refused for a long Time, after such Dissolutions, to cause others to be elected; whereby the Legislative Powers, incapable of the Annihilation, have returned to the People at large for their exercise; the State remaining in the mean time exposed to all the Dangers of Invasion from without, and the Convulsions within.

HE has endeavoured to prevent the Population of these States; for that Purpose obstructing the Laws for Naturalization of Foreigners; refusing to pass others to encourage their Migrations hither, and raising the Conditions of new Appropriations of Lands.

HE has obstructed the Administration of Justice, by refusing his Assent to Laws for establishing Judiciary Powers.

HE has made Judges dependent on his Will alone, for the Tenure of their Offices, and the Amount and Payment of their Salaries.

HE has erected a Multitude of new Offices, and sent hither Swarms of Officers to harass our People, and eat out their Substance.

HE has kept among us, in Times of Peace, Standing Armies, without the consent of our Legislatures.

HE has affected to render the Military independent of and superior to the Civil Power.

HE has combined with others to subject us to a Jurisdiction foreign to our Constitution, and unacknowledged by our Laws; giving his Assent to their Acts of pretended Legislation:

The Complete Text of the Declaration of Independence *(cont.)*

FOR quartering large Bodies of Armed Troops among us;

FOR protecting them, by a mock Trial, from Punishment for any Murders which they should commit on the Inhabitants of these States:

FOR cutting off our Trade with all Parts of the World:

FOR imposing Taxes on us without our Consent:

FOR depriving us, in many Cases, of the Benefits of Trial by Jury:

FOR transporting us beyond Seas to be tried for pretended Offences:

FOR abolishing the free System of English Laws in a neighbouring Province, establishing therein an arbitrary Government, and enlarging its Boundaries, so as to render it at once an Example and fit Instrument for introducing the same absolute Rules into these Colonies:

FOR taking away our Charters, abolishing our most valuable Laws, and altering fundamentally the Forms of our Governments:

FOR suspending our own Legislatures, and declaring themselves invested with Power to legislate for us in all Cases whatsoever.

HE has abdicated Government here, by declaring us out of his Protection and waging War against us.

HE has plundered our Seas, ravaged our Coasts, burnt our Towns, and destroyed the Lives of our People.

HE is, at this Time, transporting large Armies of foreign Mercenaries to compleat the Works of Death, Desolation, and Tyranny, already begun with circumstances of Cruelty and Perfidy, scarcely paralleled in the most barbarous Ages, and totally unworthy the Head of a civilized Nation.

HE has constrained our fellow Citizens taken Captive on the high Seas to bear Arms against their Country, to become the Executioners of their Friends and Brethren, or to fall themselves by their Hands.

HE has excited domestic Insurrections amongst us, and has endeavoured to bring on the Inhabitants of our Frontiers, the merciless Indian Savages, whose known Rule of Warfare, is an undistinguished Destruction, of all Ages, Sexes and Conditions.

IN every stage of these Oppressions we have Petitioned for Redress in the most humble Terms: Our repeated Petitions have been answered only by repeated Injury. A Prince, whose Character is thus marked by every act which may define a Tyrant, is unfit to be the Ruler of a free People.

NOR have we been wanting in Attentions to our British Brethren. We have warned them from Time to Time of Attempts by their Legislature to extend an unwarrantable Jurisdiction over us. We have reminded them of the Circumstances of our Emigration and Settlement here. We have appealed to their native Justice and Magnanimity, and we have conjured them by the Ties of our common Kindred to disavow these Usurpations, which, would inevitably interrupt our Connections and Correspondence. They too have been deaf to the Voice of Justice and of Consanguinity. We must, therefore, acquiesce in the Necessity, which denounces our Separation, and hold them, as we hold the rest of Mankind, Enemies in War, in Peace, Friends.

WE, therefore, the Representatives of the UNITED STATES OF AMERICA, in GENERAL CONGRESS, Assembled, appealing to the Supreme Judge of the World for the Rectitude of our Intentions, do, in the Name, and by Authority of the good People of these Colonies, solemnly Publish and Declare, That these United Colonies are, and of Right ought to be, FREE AND INDEPENDENT STATES; that they are absolved from all Allegiance to the British Crown, and that all political Connection between them and the State of Great-Britain, is and ought to be totally dissolved; and that as FREE AND INDEPENDENT STATES, they have full Power to levy War, conclude Peace, contract Alliances, establish Commerce, and to do all other Acts and Things which INDEPENDENT STATES may of right do. And for the support of this Declaration, with a firm Reliance on the Protection of divine Providence, we mutually pledge to each other our Lives, our Fortunes, and our sacred Honor.

Patrick Henry Speaks

Objective

√ Students will participate in a cooperative learning activity to enhance comprehension and improve expressive reading skills by engaging in reader's theater.

Materials

- copies of the speech "Give Me Liberty or Give Me Death" (page 63) for the students
- copies of *"Give Me Liberty of Give Me Death"—Reader's Theater* (page 64) for the students
- copies of *Analyzing "Give Me Liberty or Give Me Death"* (page 65) for the students
- dictionaries
- video recorder and videotape

Fluency Suggestions and Activities

You may want to complete the history and/or vocabulary activities on the following page before this fluency activity. An understanding of the historical context and vocabulary will help students analyze and read the piece fluently.

1. Read the text of "Give Me Liberty or Give Me Death" (page 63) aloud, modeling fluent reading.

2. Divide students into small groups to complete the activity sheet, *Analyzing "Give Me Liberty or Give Me Death"* (page 65). Provide them with copies of the excerpt from the speech (page 63) for reference. After completing this page, discuss their responses.

3. Explain to the students that they will read the text in the form of reader's theater. Explain that this is a shared reading activity, where several students take turns reading parts of text. Some parts of the selection are read by individual students, and some parts are read by all students.

4. Divide the students into groups of five and distribute copies of the *"Give Me Liberty or Give Me Death"—Reader's Theater* (page 64). Assign each student in the group a part to read. Parts are labeled R1 (for Reader 1) to R5. Draw their attention to the parts to be read by "All" students.

5. Have the students discuss words or phrases that should carry particular expressive emphasis. Allow students time in class to practice their readings of the text.

6. Have students present their versions of the reading to class. Then, arrange to make a video of the students' presentations and send the tape to a convalescent home in your school's neighborhood. Have students write letters to the people living there explaining their project. You may want to time these presentations to celebrate the anniversary of the speech, which was given on March 23, 1775.

Patrick Henry Speaks (cont.)

History Connection

Begin the lesson by introducing Patrick Henry and discussing the historical information provided below. Then, read the title of the text selection and ask them to discuss the concept of *liberty* by asking the following questions: What does liberty mean to you? Why is liberty important to us today? In Henry's time, why do you think people wanted liberty? Next, ask the students to consider the phrase, "Give Me Liberty of Give Me Death." Ask them why a person might want death if he or she could not have liberty.

Just weeks before the outbreak of the Revolutionary War, on March 23, 1775, Patrick Henry, one of the greatest speakers of the eighteenth century, addressed the Virginia House of Burgesses. Responding to legislators who still wanted to work for peace with the British, he concluded with remarks that still speak to people today. He included in his speech many biblical and religious references as was common for that time. These references point out the efforts of the British government to bind the colonies with repressive laws. Henry brings his audience to the inevitable conclusion that war is coming and there remains no choice about the matter.

Vocabulary Connection

Discuss unfamiliar vocabulary encountered in the text. Some possible words are listed below. After identifying the difficult words, discuss them within the context of the text.

- **presides**—watches over and guides
- **destinies**—futures
- **vigilant**—someone who watches carefully in order to avoid danger
- **base**—without high values and morals
- **retreat**—to move back
- **submission**—to give up
- **forged**—made
- **inevitable**—something that cannot be avoided
- **vain**—no use
- **extenuate**—make light of
- **gale**—wind or movement
- **brethren**—people who fight for the same thing as you
- **idle**—doing nothing

Extension Idea

- Invite students who would like a greater challenge to practice and possibly memorize Patrick Henry's speech. Encourage them to recite the lines of the speech with great conviction and confidence.

Give Me Liberty or Give Me Death

This is an excerpt from a famous speech by Patrick Henry.

There is a just God who presides over the destinies of nations, and who will raise up friends to fight our battles for us. The battle, sir, is not to the strong alone; it is to the vigilant, the active, the brave. Besides, sir, we have no election. If we were base enough to desire it, it is now too late to retire from the contest. There is no retreat but in submission and slavery! Our chains are forged! Their clanking may be heard on the plains of Boston! The war is inevitable—and let it come! I repeat it, sir, let it come.

It is in vain, sir, to extenuate the matter. Gentlemen may cry, Peace, Peace—but there is no peace. The war is actually begun! The next gale that sweeps from the north will bring to our ears the clash of resounding arms! Our brethren are already in the field! Why stand we here idle? What is it that gentlemen wish? What would they have? Is life so dear, or peace so sweet, as to be purchased at the price of chains and slavery? Forbid it, Almighty God! I know not what course others may take; but as for me, give me liberty or give me death!

"Give Me Liberty or Give Me Death"— Reader's Theater

R1:   There is a just God who presides over the destinies of nations, and who will raise up friends to fight our battles for us.

R2:   The battle, sir, is not to the strong alone;

R3:   it is to the vigilant,

R4:   the active,

R5:   the brave.

R1:   Besides, sir, we have no election.

R2:   If we were base enough to desire it, it is now too late to retire from the contest.

R3:   There is no retreat but in submission and slavery!

All: **Our chains are forged!**

R4:   Their clanking may be heard on the plains of Boston!

R5:   The war is inevitable—and let it come! I repeat it, sir,

All: **let it come.**

R1:   It is in vain, sir, to extenuate the matter.

R2:   Gentlemen may cry,

All: **Peace, Peace—**

R3:   but there is no peace. The war is actually begun!

R4:   The next gale that sweeps from the north will bring to our ears the clash of resounding arms!

R5:   Our brethren are already in the field! Why stand we here idle?

R1:   What is it that gentlemen wish?

R2:   What would they have?

R3:   Is life so dear, or peace so sweet, as to be purchased at the price of chains and slavery?

All: **Forbid it, Almighty God!**

R4:   I know not what course others may take;

R5:   but as for me,

All: **give me liberty or give me death!**

Name_____

Analyzing "Give Me Liberty or Give Me Death"

Directions: Meet with your classmates to answer the questions below.

1. Define the following words:

   - presides— _____
   - inevitable— _____
   - vain—_____
   - gale—_____
   - liberty— _____

2. What does Patrick Henry mean when he says "There is no retreat but in submission and slavery!"?

   _____

   _____

3. Interpret the following statement: "The next gale that sweeps from the north will bring to our ears the clash of resounding arms!"

   _____

   _____

   _____

4. To what war does Henry refer?

   _____

5. Why is liberty so important to Henry?

   _____

   _____

   _____

   _____

Yankee Doodle Dandy

Objective

√ Students will deliver a group oral presentation and read passages fluently with changes in tone, voice, timing, and expression using echo reading.

Materials

- copies of "Yankee Doodle" lyrics (page 68) for the students
- copies of *"Yankee Doodle"—Divided* (page 69) for the students
- optional: copies of *Analyzing "Yankee Doodle"* (page 70) for the students
- optional: tape recorder and recording of the song

Fluency Suggestions and Activities

You may want to complete the history and/or vocabulary activities on the following page before this fluency activity. An understanding of the historical context and vocabulary will help students analyze and read the piece fluently.

1. Give each student a copy of the "Yankee Doodle" lyrics (page 68). Read the song aloud, modeling fluent reading. If possible, have students listen to a recording of the song after your reading. Also provided is the *Full Text of "Yankee Doodle"* (page 71), if you would like your students to follow along with the recording.

2. Read the poem as an echo reading with the class. You read two lines and the students read them back to you. Continue until you have read the entire poem.

3. Ask students to look for clues in the text that tell them how to read it (e.g., commas, exclamation marks, periods, or repetition).

4. Place the students into groups of four. Each group will be responsible for presenting an echo reading to the class. Then, the class will vote on which group gave the most energetic and interesting performance. If you want to, you could assign specific roles to these groups. One group could act as the British using the song to taunt the colonists. The other could say the song as colonists who adopted the song as their own. This gives them real reasons for the tones and inflections they will use.

5. Once the students are in their groups, give them copies of *"Yankee Doodle"—Divided* (page 69). This sheet has the piece broken into echo reading parts for four students. Any groups that have more than or fewer than four students will need to alter their assignment so that every student participates (e.g., two students read together, students read fewer lines, students read more lines).

6. On the day of the presentations, have each group perform its echo reading. Encourage students to use hand motions and facial expressions as they read. Remind them that they want to get the audience involved in the presentation of the song. Then, after all the groups have presented, take a vote on which group gave the most energetic and interesting performance. You might want to tell students that they cannot vote for their own groups.

Yankee Doodle Dandy (cont.)

History Connection

Discuss the history of the poem using the information below.

Everyone knows the song "Yankee Doodle," but no one knows who wrote it. Most musical historians agree that it was composed in the 1750s. In 1755, a British soldier sang the song while he was making fun of tired, dirty American soldiers who fought with the British against the French and Indians. The song makes fun of Americans for thinking that a feather was as attractive as a macaroni hairstyle. Twenty years later, American soldiers fighting in the Revolutionary War sang the song as they marched into battle against the British. Bands played it at sites of military victories, and the song became an unofficial national anthem.

Vocabulary Connection

Discuss unfamiliar vocabulary encountered in the text. Some possible words are listed below. After identifying the difficult words, discuss them within the context of the text.

- **Yankee**—a term for people from New England
- **doodle**—another word for fool
- **cap**—a type of hat
- **macaroni**—the tall hairstyle worn by fashionable people in London
- **dandy**—a person who spends a lot of time making sure they look good
- **handy**—clever
- **hasty pudding**—a British porridge

Extension Ideas

- Discuss the meaning of the poem for comprehension and further analyze the lyrics. Ask what "went to town," "mind the music and the step," "with the girls be handy" mean. Find out who Captain Gooding was. Then, group students in pairs. Have them complete the activity sheet, *Analyzing "Yankee Doodle"* (page 70) together.

- Divide the class into four groups. Assign the first, third, and fifth stanzas to three groups. Assign the refrain to the fourth group. Students will practice reading the poem aloud and perform it for other classes. They can design props such as coonskin caps with a feather stuck in them, a uniform for Washington, or characters dressed in period clothing. You might even want to find a recipe for hasty pudding to try. Other historic patriotic songs could be included in the presentation as well.

Yankee Doodle

Yankee doodle went to town,
A-riding on a pony,
He stuck a feather in his cap
And called it macaroni!

Yankee doodle, keep it up,
Yankee doodle dandy;
Mind the music and the step,
And with the girls be handy.

Father and I went down to camp,
Along with Captain Gooding;
And there we saw the men and boys,
As thick as hasty pudding.

Yankee doodle, keep it up,
Yankee doodle dandy;
Mind the music and the step,
And with the girls be handy.

There was Captain Washington
Upon a slapping stallion,
A-giving orders to his men,
I guess there was a million.

Yankee doodle, keep it up,
Yankee doodle dandy;
Mind the music and the step,
And with the girls be handy.

Name _____

"Yankee Doodle"—Divided

Student 1

Yankee doodle went to town,

A-riding on a pony,

(Audience echoes)

Student 2

He stuck a feather in his cap

And called it macaroni!

(Audience echoes)

All together

Yankee doodle, keep it up,

Yankee doodle dandy;

Mind the music and the step,

And with the girls be handy.

Student 3

Father and I went down to camp,

Along with Captain Gooding;

(Audience echoes)

Student 4

And there we saw the men and boys,

As thick as hasty pudding.

(Audience echoes)

All together

Yankee doodle, keep it up,

Yankee doodle dandy;

Mind the music and the step,

And with the girls be handy.

Students 1 and 2

There was Captain Washington

Upon a slapping stallion,

(Audience echoes)

Students 3 and 4

A-giving orders to his men,

I guess there was a million.

(Audience echoes)

All together

Yankee doodle, keep it up,

Yankee doodle dandy;

Mind the music and the step,

And with the girls be handy.

Name _____

Analyzing "Yankee Doodle"

Directions: Answer the following questions.

1. In this song the author called the colonists "Yankee doodles." In your own words, explain what this means. _____

_____

_____

_____

2. When reading this song, what should you do when you come to a comma?
   a. read a little louder
   b. read a little faster
   c. pause briefly

3. How did the colonists react to this song?

_____

_____

_____

_____

4. Read this song twice with a partner. On the first reading, read as if you were British. On the second reading, read as if you were a Patriot. Have your partner list any changes in your tone, volume, or reading rate in the chart below.

Character	Tone	Volume	Reading Rate
British soldier			
Patriot			

Full Text of "Yankee Doodle"

Yankee doodle went to town,
A-riding on a pony,
He stuck a feather in his cap
And called it macaroni!

Yankee doodle, keep it up,
Yankee doodle dandy;
Mind the music and the step,
And with the girls be handy.

Father and I went down to camp,
Along with Captain Gooding;
And there we saw the men and boys,
As thick as hasty pudding.

There was Captain Washington
Upon a slapping stallion,
A-giving orders to his men,
I guess there was a million.

And then the feathers on his hat,
They looked so' tarnal fin-a,
I wanted pockily to get
To give to my Jemima.

And then we saw a swamping gun,
Large as a log of maple;
Upon a deuced little cart,
A load for father's cattle.

And every time they shoot it off,
It takes a horn of powder;
It makes a noise like father's gun,
Only a nation louder.

I went as nigh to one myself,
As' Siah's underpinning;
And father went as nigh agin,
I thought the deuce was in him.

We saw a little barrel, too,
The heads were made of leather;
They knocked upon it with little clubs,
And called the folks together.

And there they'd fife away like fun,
And play on cornstalk fiddles,
And some had ribbons red as blood,
All bound around their middles.

The troopers, too, would gallop up
And fire right in our faces;
It scared me almost to death
To see them run such races.

Uncle Sam came there to change
Some pancakes and some onions,
For' lasses cake to carry home
To give his wife and young ones.

But I can't tell half I see
They kept up such a smother;
So I took my hat off, made a bow,
And scampered home to mother.

Cousin Simon grew so bold,
I thought he would have cocked it;
It scared me so I streaked it off,
And hung by father's pocket.

And there I saw a pumpkin shell,
As big as mother's basin;
And every time they touched it off,
They scampered like the nation.

Yankee doodle, keep it up,
Yankee doodle dandy;
Mind the music and the step,
And with the girls be handy

Paul Revere's Famous Night

Objective

√ Students will read aloud fluently and accurately with changes in tone, voice, timing, and expression using the strategy of choral reading.

Materials

- copies of *Excerpt from "Paul Revere's Ride"* (page 74) for the students
- copies of *The Refrain from "Paul Revere's Ride"* (page 75) for the students

Fluency Suggestions and Activities

You may want to complete the history and/or vocabulary activities on the following page before this fluency activity. An understanding of the historical context and vocabulary will help students analyze and read the piece fluently.

1. Give each student a copy of *Excerpt from "Paul Revere's Ride"* (page 74). Read the selection aloud modeling fluent reading. (Also provided is the *Full Text of "Paul Revere's Ride"* (pages 76–77) if you would like your students to read the entire poem.)

2. Then, read the poem with the entire class as a choral reading. You may want to stop reading after each stanza the first time you read the poem. Slowing the pace will help keep the students reading with you. Next, have students get into small groups and practice reading the poem chorally with their groups. Then read the poem a third time with the entire class all reading at the same time.

3. Distribute and introduce *The Refrain from "Paul Revere's Ride"* (page 75). Model how you want the students to read it. Use a great deal of expression and change the volume for a dramatic effect:

   - Read in a normal volume, read again a little softer, and then fade to a whisper.
   - After fading to a whisper, gradually increase the volume.
   - Add sound effects by having students clap and slap knees to mimic the sound of a horse's hooves.

4. Within their small groups, have the students develop their own unique way of reading the refrain of the poem. Give them ample time to practice their choral reading of the refrain piece.

5. After student groups have developed and practiced their presentations of the refrain, have each group perform for the class. Once all the groups have performed, have students choose the group that gave the best performance.

6. Finally, perform a full-class reading of the poem. Have the chosen group perform the refrain in place of the first stanza. Then, the rest of the class reads the next stanza chorally. In between each stanza, the refrain group performs its masterpiece. If that group included sound effects in its reading, you may choose to allow the other students in the class to join in for the clapping or stomping.

Paul Revere's Famous Night (cont.)

History Connection

Begin with a brief discussion of Paul Revere and his role in the years before the American Revolution. The information below will give you some background on the subject.

Paul Revere is best known for his famous ride through the countryside to warn the minutemen that the British soldiers had arrived. During the years before the war, Revere was an important figure in the politics of Boston. Revere was a Patriot and a member of the Sons of Liberty. This group protested taxes and the actions of King George III. He supported the group both financially, and through his own participation in many of the boycotts and rebellious actions in the 1760s and 1770s. On the night of his famous ride, the British captured him. He was later set free and continued to contribute to the war effort.

Vocabulary Connection

Discuss unfamiliar vocabulary encountered in the text. Some possible words are listed below. After identifying the difficult words, discuss them within the context of the text.

- **aloft**—high in the air
- **belfry**—the bell tower on a church
- **muffled**—when something is wrapped up so it does not make as much noise
- **muster**—gathering of a group of people
- **barrack**—a large building usually used for housing soldiers
- **tread**—footsteps
- **grenadiers**—soldiers who are armed with grenades
- **spurred**—had pointed metal connected to one's boots
- **impetuous**—strong and violent
- **spectral**—like a ghost
- **sombre**—something that is dark, gloomy, and serious
- **gleam**—the small or faint appearance of light
- **defiance**—resistance
- **peril**—danger

Extension Idea

- Have students list the causes (sequence of events) leading up to Paul Revere's ride (end result or effect). Some research may need to be done to answer any questions generated by students. They may want to find out who "his friend" was or check a map of Boston to locate the Charles River or the Old North Church.

Excerpt from "Paul Revere's Ride"

By Henry Wadsworth Longfellow

Listen, my children, and you shall hear
Of the midnight ride of Paul Revere,
On the eighteenth of April, in Seventy-five;
Hardly a man is now alive
Who remembers that famous day and year.

He said to his friend, "If the British march
By land or sea from the town to-night,
Hang a lantern aloft in the belfry arch
Of the North Church tower as a signal light,—
One, if by land, and two, if by sea;
And I on the opposite shore will be,
Ready to ride and spread the alarm
Through every Middlesex village and farm
For the country folk to be up and to arm," . . .

Then he said, "Good night!" and with muffled oar
Silently rowed to the Charlestown shore, . . .

Meanwhile, his friend, through alley and street,
Wanders and watches with eager ears,
Till in the silence around him he hears
The muster of men at the barrack door,
The sound of arms, and the tramp of feet,
And the measured tread of the grenadiers,
Marching down to their boats on the shore . . .

Meanwhile, impatient to mount and ride,
Booted and spurred, with a heavy stride
On the opposite shore walked Paul Revere.
Now he patted his horse's side,
Now gazed at the landscape far and near,
Then, impetuous, stamped the earth,

And turned and tightened his saddle-girth;
But mostly he watched with eager search
The belfry-tower of the Old North Church,
As it rose above the graves on the hill,
Lonely and spectral and sombre and still.
And lo! as he looks, on the belfry's height
A glimmer, and then a gleam of light!
He springs to the saddle, the bridle he turns,
But lingers and gazes, till full on his sight
A second lamp in the belfry burns! . . .

You know the rest. In the books you have read,
How the British Regulars fired and fled,—
How the farmers gave them ball for ball,
From behind each fence and farm-yard wall,
Chasing the red-coats down the lane,
Then crossing the fields to emerge again
Under the trees at the turn of the road,
And only pausing to fire and load.

So through the night rode Paul Revere;
And so through the night went his cry of alarm
To every Middlesex village and farm,—
A cry of defiance and not of fear,
A voice in the darkness, a knock at the door,
And a word that shall echo forevermore!
For, borne on the night-wind of the Past,
Through all our history, to the last,
In the hour of darkness and peril and need,
The people will waken and listen to hear
The hurrying hoof-beats of that steed,
And the midnight message of Paul Revere.

Name _____

The Refrain from "Paul Revere's Ride"

Listen my children
Listen, listen, (*softer*)

And you shall hear
Listen, listen, (*softer*)

Of the midnight ride
Of the midnight ride (*softer*)

Of Paul Revere
Of Paul Revere (*softer*)
Listen, listen, (*softer*)

Listen my children and you shall hear
Of the midnight ride of Paul Revere
Listen, listen (*softer*)

Full Text of "Paul Revere's Ride"

By Henry Wadsworth Longfellow

Listen, my children, and you shall hear
Of the midnight ride of Paul Revere,
On the eighteenth of April, in Seventy-five;
Hardly a man is now alive
Who remembers that famous day and year.

He said to his friend, "If the British march
By land or sea from the town to-night,
Hang a lantern aloft in the belfry arch
Of the North Church tower as a signal light,—
One, if by land, and two, if by sea;
And I on the opposite shore will be,
Ready to ride and spread the alarm
Through every Middlesex village and farm
For the country folk to be up and to arm,"

Then he said, "Good night!" and with muffled oar
Silently rowed to the Charlestown shore,
Just as the moon rose over the bay,
Where swinging wide at her moorings lay
The Somerset, British man-of-war;
A phantom ship, with each mast and spar
Across the moon like a prison bar,
And a huge black hulk, that was magnified
By its own reflection in the tide.

Meanwhile, his friend, through alley and street,
Wanders and watches with eager ears,
Till in the silence around him he hears
The muster of men at the barrack door,
The sound of arms, and the tramp of feet,
And the measured tread of the grenadiers,
Marching down to their boats on the shore.

Then he climbed the tower of the Old North Church,
By the wooden stairs, with stealthy tread,
To the belfry-chamber overhead,
And startled the pigeons from their perch
On the sombre rafters, that round him made
Masses and moving shapes of shade,—

By the trembling ladder, steep and tall
To the highest window in the wall,
Where he paused to listen and look down
A moment on the roofs of the town,
And the moonlight flowing over all.

Beneath, in the churchyard, lay the dead,
In their night-encampment on the hill,
Wrapped in silence so deep and still
That he could hear, like a sentinel's tread,
The watchful night-wind, as it went
Creeping along from tent to tent
And seeming to whisper, "All is well!"
A moment only he feels the spell
Of the place and the hour, and the secret dread
Of the lonely belfry and the dead;
For suddenly all his thoughts are bent
On a shadowy something far away,
Where the river widens to meet the bay,—
A line of black that bends and floats
On the rising tide, like a bridge of boats.

Meanwhile, impatient to mount and ride,
Booted and spurred, with a heavy stride
On the opposite shore walked Paul Revere.
Now he patted his horse's side,
Now gazed at the landscape far and near,
Then, impetuous, stamped the earth,
And turned and tightened his saddle-girth;
But mostly he watched with eager search
The belfry-tower of the Old North Church,
As it rose above the graves on the hill,
Lonely and spectral and sombre and still.
And lo! as he looks, on the belfry's height
A glimmer, and then a gleam of light!
He springs to the saddle, the bridle he turns,
But lingers and gazes, till full on his sight
A second lamp in the belfry burns!

Full Text of "Paul Revere's Ride" *(cont.)*

A hurry of hoofs in a village street,
A shape in the moonlight, a bulk in the dark,
And beneath, from the pebbles, in passing,
a spark
Struck out by a steed flying fearless and fleet:
That was all! And yet, through the gloom and the
light,
The fate of a nation was riding that night;
And the spark struck out by that steed, in
his flight,
Kindled the land into flame with its heat.
He has left the village and mounted the steep,
And beneath him, tranquil and broad and deep,
Is the Mystic, meeting the ocean tides;
And under the alders, that skirt its edge,
Now soft on the sand, now loud on the ledge,
Is heard the tramp of his steed as he rides.

It was twelve by the village clock
When he crossed the bridge into Medford town.
He heard the crowing of the cock,
And the barking of the farmer's dog,
And felt the damp of the river fog,
That rises after the sun goes down.

It was one by the village clock,
When he galloped into Lexington.
He saw the gilded weathercock
Swim in the moonlight as he passed,
And the meeting-house windows, blank
and bare,
Gaze at him with a spectral glare,
As if they already stood aghast
At the bloody work they would look upon.

It was two by the village clock,
When he came to the bridge in Concord town.
He heard the bleating of the flock,
And the twitter of birds among the trees,
And felt the breath of the morning breeze
Blowing over the meadows brown.
And one was safe and asleep in his bed
Who at the bridge would be first to fall,
Who that day would be lying dead,
Pierced by a British musket-ball.

You know the rest. In the books you have read,
How the British Regulars fired and fled,—
How the farmers gave them ball for ball,
From behind each fence and farm-yard wall,
Chasing the red-coats down the lane,
Then crossing the fields to emerge again
Under the trees at the turn of the road,
And only pausing to fire and load.

So through the night rode Paul Revere;
And so through the night went his cry of alarm
To every Middlesex village and farm,—
A cry of defiance and not of fear,
A voice in the darkness, a knock at the door,
And a word that shall echo forevermore!
For, borne on the night-wind of the Past,
Through all our history, to the last,
In the hour of darkness and peril and need,
The people will waken and listen to hear
The hurrying hoof-beats of that steed,
And the midnight message of Paul Revere.

Paine's Common Sense

Objective

√ Students will deliver a group oral presentation and read passages fluently after practicing and monitoring fluency with repeated readings.

Materials

- copy of *Excerpt from Common Sense* (page 80) for the teacher
- copies of *Common Sense—Divided Reading* (pages 81–82) for the students

Fluency Suggestions and Activities

You may want to complete the history and/or vocabulary activities on the following page before this fluency activity. An understanding of the historical context and vocabulary will help students analyze and read the piece fluently.

1. Read the *Excerpt from Common Sense* (page 80) aloud, demonstrating fluent reading with attention to accuracy, voice tone, and expression. After the reading, explain that difficult texts require practice to improve fluency. To do this, repeated readings are very helpful. Explain to students that they will have the opportunity to read portions of the text several times and monitor their progress with each reading. Write the following on the board:

   First Reading:

   Second Reading:

   Third Reading:

2. Explain that after each reading, they will each reflect on their progress and write a comment about it. Demonstrate this process by reading the following passage. (After reading, you might write a comment, such as, "Pretty good, but I made a few mistakes.")

   > To the evil of monarchy we have added that of hereditary succession; and as the first is a degradation and lessening of ourselves, so the second, claimed as a matter of right, is an insult and an imposition on posterity.

3. Read the passage again. Then, write a second comment, such as, "Much better, but I was still a little bit slow."

4. Read the text for a final time and write the third comment, such as, "This was my best reading, but I still need to practice."

5. Divide the students into groups of two or three. Then, distribute copies of *Common Sense—Divided Reading* (page 81) to students. Have students assign passages to group members. Each student should have at least two passages to practice.

6. Allow the students time in class to practice their readings. Each time they practice, they should write comments about their progress. Encourage them to continue repeated readings beyond the first three times to increase fluency. Once the students are comfortable with their fluency, have the entire group practice reading the text in sequence.

7. Arrange presentations of *Common Sense* for other classes in the school. Be sure to have one of the group members provide a brief history of the text before their presentations.

Paine's Common Sense (cont.)

History Connection

Discuss the history of *Common Sense* using the information below.

Thomas Paine was a Patriot during the years leading up to the American Revolution. Not only did he believe that the colonists had a right to protest the actions of the British, but he believed the colonists should declare their independence from Great Britian. He is best known for writing *Common Sense* in 1776. This pamphlet was propaganda to convince people to declare independence from Britain. *Common Sense* stated that America needed its own government. He wanted a government that could serve all the people. The excerpt to be read here tries to explain the folly of hereditary titles.

Vocabulary Connection

Discuss unfamiliar vocabulary encountered in the text. Some possible words are listed below. After identifying the difficult words, discuss them within the context of the text.

- **monarchy**—when a single person (e.g., a king or queen) rules a country
- **hereditary**—when something (like the title of king) is passed between family members
- **succession**—things that happen one after another
- **degradation**—when you lose some of your self worth
- **posterity**—future generations
- **perpetual**—going on forever
- **contemporaries**—people who are about the same age as each other
- **folly**—when something is not sensible
- **bestowed**—to be given something as a gift
- **manifest injustice**—obvious wrongdoing
- **rogue**—a person who is dishonest
- **sentiments**—thoughts
- **contempt**—to dislike and disrespect something
- **plunder**—things that have been stolen or taken without permission

Extension Idea

- Remind students that Thomas Paine's document was intended to bring about change. Ask the students to think about something at their school that they would like to see changed. Instruct them to write their own speeches concerning the selected issues. Encourage them to use repeated readings to practice their speeches before presenting them to the class, other classes in school, and/or to the principal.

Excerpt from Common Sense

By Thomas Paine

To the evil of monarchy we have added that of hereditary succession; and as the first is a degradation and lessening of ourselves, so the second, claimed as a matter of right, is an insult and an imposition on posterity. For all men being originally equals, no ONE by BIRTH could have a right to set up his own family in perpetual preference to all others for ever, and though himself might deserve SOME decent degree of honours of his contemporaries, yet his descendants might be far too unworthy to inherit them.

Secondly, as no man at first could possess any other public honours than were bestowed upon him, so the givers of those honours could have no power to give away the right of posterity. And though they might say, "We chose you for OUR head," they could not, without manifest injustice to their children, say, "that your children and your children's children shall reign over OURS for ever." Because such an unwise, unjust, unnatural compact might (perhaps) in the next succession put them under the government of a rogue or a fool. Most wise men, in their private sentiments, have ever treated hereditary right with contempt; yet it is one of those evils, which when once established is not easily removed; many submit from fear, others from superstition, and the more powerful part shares with the king the plunder of the rest.

Name _____

Common Sense—Divided Reading

To the evil of monarchy we have added that of hereditary succession; and as the first is a degradation and lessening of ourselves, so the second, claimed as a matter of right, is an insult and an imposition on posterity.

Comments:

First Reading: _____

Second Reading: _____

Third Reading: _____

For all men being originally equals, no ONE by BIRTH could have a right to set up his own family in perpetual preference to all others for ever, and though himself might deserve SOME decent degree of honours of his contemporaries, yet his descendants might be far too unworthy to inherit them.

Comments:

First Reading: _____

Second Reading: _____

Third Reading: _____

Secondly, as no man at first could possess any other public honours than were bestowed upon him, so the givers of those honours could have no power to give away the right of posterity.

Comments:

First Reading: _____

Second Reading: _____

Third Reading: _____

Common Sense—Divided Reading (cont.)

And though they might say, "We chose you for OUR head," they could not, without manifest injustice to their children, say, "that your children and your children's children shall reign over OURS for ever."

Comments:

First Reading: _____

Second Reading: _____

Third Reading: _____

Because such an unwise, unjust, unnatural compact might (perhaps) in the next succession put them under the government of a rogue or a fool.

Comments:

First Reading: _____

Second Reading: _____

Third Reading: _____

Most wise men, in their private sentiments, have ever treated hereditary right with contempt; yet it is one of those evils, which when once established is not easily removed; many submit from fear, others from superstition, and the more powerful part shares with the king the plunder of the rest.

Comments:

First Reading: _____

Second Reading: _____

Third Reading: _____

July 4, 1788

Objective

√ Students will perform a choral reading of a passage, paying close attention to their changes in tone, voice, timing, and expression.

Materials

- copies of the poem "An Ode for the 4th of July 1788" (page 85) for the students
- copies of *Analyzing "An Ode for the 4th of July 1788"* (page 86) for the students

Fluency Suggestions and Activities

You may want to complete the history and/or vocabulary activities on the following page before this fluency activity. An understanding of the historical context and vocabulary will help students analyze and read the piece fluently.

Note: Before beginning the lesson, practice reading "An Ode for the 4th of July 1788" (page 85) until you are able to read it smoothly and accurately.

1. Read the poem, "An Ode for the 4th of July 1788" (page 85), aloud modeling fluent reading. Explain to the students that developing fluency isn't just about practicing one's own fluent reading. It also involves listening to other readers.

2. Explain to the students that when reading poetry it is necessary to use proper phrasing. Define phrasing as chunking together groups of words. Without proper phrasing, poetry can be difficult to understand. Demonstrate how phrasing is used in "An Ode for the 4th of July 1788" by writing the first two lines on the board. Read the lines in a choppy manner without the use of expression. Ask the students to tell what is wrong with the way you have recited the words.

   OH for a muse of sire! to mount the skies
   And to a listn'ing world proclaim—

3. Write the next two lines on the chalkboard and add slash marks (see below) in appropriate places to indicate pauses for phrasing. Instruct the students to read the lines along with you. Explain that the words before the slash should be chunked together and the words after the slash should be chunked. So the reading would sound like this: Behold! (pause) behold! (pause) an empire rise! (pause) An Era new, (pause) Time, (pause) as he flies,

   Behold! / behold! / an empire rise! /
   An Era new, / Time, / as he flies,

4. Next, provide each student with a copy of the poem (page 85). Explain that this poem may be difficult to read, but with repeated practice, it will get easier.

5. Divide the students into four groups. Assign one stanza to each group. Allow them time to practice reciting their assigned stanzas of the poem together. After a few days of practice, have all the groups read their stanzas in order. In this way, the class con perform the whole poem together.

July 4, 1788 *(cont.)*

History Connection

Discuss the Constitutional Convention and the years from 1776 to 1787. The information below gives some information about this time period.

After the Revolutionary War, the Continental Congress wrote America's first system of rules. These rules were called the Articles of Confederation. These rules did not give anyone enough power to do what needed to be done. The new country was in a lot of trouble. Representatives from the different colonies held a meeting to rewrite the document. By the time they finished, they had made so many changes that it got a new name. It was called the Constitution of the United States of America.

Vocabulary Connection

Discuss unfamiliar vocabulary encountered in the text. Some possible words are listed below. After identifying the difficult words, discuss them within the context of the text.

- **ode**—a type of poem written to honor someone or something
- **muse**—something that inspires
- **Alleghany's**—mountains in Pennsylvania and Virginia
- **tidings**—news
- **decrees**—orders
- **plaudit**—clapping in agreement
- **valiant**—when someone is brave
- **commerce**—business
- **pond'rous**—ponderous, something that is very heavy
- **vain**—to do something and not be successful
- **array'd**—arrayed, to be dressed in something

Extension Idea

- Discuss the meanings of the words with unusual spellings, such as: listn'ing, enter'd, tow'ring, o'er, num'rous, Heav'n, gen'ral, pond'rous, and array'd. Display these words on the board and ask the students to determine the pronunciation of each. Explain that while these words may seem unfamiliar at first glance, most are familiar words, when spelled in a conventional manner. They are often spelled this way in poems and song lyrics for the purposes of flow and rhythm.

- Then, have the students complete the activity page, *Analyzing "An Ode for the 4th of July 1788"* (page 86), addressing their questions about the poem. After students have completed the page, allow them to have a question/answer session with you and the rest of the class to discuss their questions.

An Ode for the 4th of July 1788

OH for a muse of sire! to mount the skies
And to a listn'ing world proclaim—
Behold! behold! an empire rise!
An Era new, Time, as he flies,
Hath enter'd in the book of fame.
On Alleghany's tow'ring head
Echo shall stand—the tidings spread,
And o'er the lakes, and misty floods around,
An ERA NEW resound.

See! where Columbia sits alone,
And from her star-bespangled throne,
Beholds the gay procession move along,
And hears the trumpet, and the choral song—
She hears her sons rejoice—
Looks into future times, and sees
The num'rous blessings Heav'n decrees,
And with HER plaudit joins the gen'ral voice.

"Tis done! tis done! my Sons," she cries,
"In War are valiant, and in Council wise;
"Wisdom and Valour shall my rights defend,
"And o'er my vast domain those rights extend.
"Science shall flourish—Genius stretch her wing,
"In native Strains Columbian Muses sing;
"Wealth crown the Arts, and Justice clean her scales,
"Commerce her pond'rous anchor weigh,
"Wide spread her fails,
"And in far distant seas her flag display.

"My sons for Freedom fought, nor fought in vain;
"But found a naked goddess was their gain:
"Good government alone, can shew the Maid,
"In robes of SOCIAL HAPPINESS array'd."
Hail to this festival! all hail the day!
Columbia's standard on HER ROOF display:
And let the PEOPLE'S Motto ever be,

**"UNITED THUS, and
THUS UNITED-FREE."**

Source: The Library of Congress

Name _____

Analyzing "An Ode for the 4th of July 1788"

Directions: Answer the following questions.

1. What words in the poem are unfamiliar to you? Take a guess at the meaning of each.

Word	Meaning	Word	Meaning

2. Read each stanza of the poem and determine the general message.

Stanza 1: _____

Stanza 2: _____

Stanza 3: _____

Stanza 4: _____

3. Think of a slogan (or a few sentences) that summarize the overall message of the poem.

_____

_____

_____

_____

Preamble to the Constitution

Objective

√ Students will participate in cooperative learning and improve expressive reading skills by engaging in reader's theater.

Materials

- copy of the *Preamble to the Constitution* (page 89) for the teacher
- copies of *Preamble to the Constitution Reader's Theater* (pages 90–91) for the students
- highlighters
- optional: manila paper, markers, and tape for the Extension Idea

Fluency Suggestions and Activities

You may want to complete the history and/or vocabulary activities on the following page before this fluency activity. An understanding of the historical context and vocabulary will help students analyze and read the piece fluently.

Note: You might want to plan to complete this fluency activity around September 17, which is Constitution Day.

1. Model a fluent reading of the *Preamble to the Constitution* (page 89) for the students.

2. Give each student a copy of *Preamble to the Constitution Reader's Theater* (pages 90–91). Place students into groups of seven. Assign parts to students by having them volunteer or audition. Have students highlight their parts.

3. Read the script together (choral reading) several times. Model reading lines with changes in pitch, tone, and timing to achieve different effects. Ask students to look for clues in the text that tell them how to read it (e.g., commas, bold type for emphasis).

4. Students then begin to read their assigned parts aloud. Provide time for practice individually, with partners, and in small groups.

5. Students should then practice their parts with their whole groups. Once the students are comfortable, have them perform their readings to classrooms of younger students.

Preamble to the Constitution *(cont.)*

History Connection

Discuss the history of the Preamble using the information below.

The first 52 words in the Constitution are called the Preamble. These words explain why the Constitution was written. Americans wanted a more "perfect union." That means that the states would have to act as a team so the country could be great. The Articles of Confederation did not help the states work together very well.

The colonists were angry about how King George III had treated them. When they made the new government, the colonists wanted to make sure the laws were fair for all people in America. Americans wanted peace in their new land. They thought the government should protect the people from harm by providing safety from all enemies. The Americans wrote the Constitution so they could be free forever.

Vocabulary Connection

Discuss unfamiliar vocabulary encountered in the text. Some possible words are listed below. After identifying the difficult words, discuss them within the context of the text.

- **insure**—to make certain
- **tranquility**—when things are peaceful and calm
- **welfare**—the conditions that people live in
- **posterity**—future generations
- **ordain**—to start something officially
- **amended**—to change something
- **indigo**—a color, purple

Extension Idea

- Provide manila paper, markers, pens, lined writing paper (if you wish a handwritten piece), and tape. Divide the Preamble into eight phrases. Assign several students to each phrase of the Preamble. Give each student a sheet of paper to draw an illustration to accompany each phrase. Students will write brief explanations of their illustrations as they pertain to the phrases. Ask them to include examples of how the government makes provisions for establishing justice, ensuring domestic tranquility, and so on, today. Have students write a document on the computer and print it or write on the lined paper. When all of the pages have been completed, lay them out and form a Preamble quilt. Tape the sheets together and display the quilt.

Preamble to the Constitution

We the People of the United States, in Order to form a more perfect Union, establish Justice, insure domestic Tranquility, provide for the common defense, promote the general Welfare, and secure the Blessings of Liberty to ourselves and our Posterity, do ordain and establish this Constitution for the United States of America.

Name _____

Preamble to the Constitution Reader's Theater

R1:   The Constitution of the United States describes the plan of our government

R2:   and the rights of the American people.

R3:   It contains 4,543 words.

R4:   It is a living document

R5:   which means it can be changed or amended.

R6:   This has only been done 27 times.

R7:   It is more powerful than any branch of government

R1:   or any state in the Union.

R2:   The first part of the Constitution is the Preamble.

R3:   A preamble is an introduction

R4:   where the document and its purpose are explained.

All: We the people of the United States,

R5:   came here from England, Scotland, France, Sweden, and Holland

R6:   Mary, Elizabeth, Sarah, and Hannah

R7:   William, Richard, Patrick, and Edward

R1:   We came to New England to find religious freedom

R2:   and to farm and fish.

R3:   We grew corn and wheat in Rhode Island, Connecticut, Massachusetts, and New Hampshire.

R4:   We came to practice our own religion and to make money in the middle colonies.

R5:   Many of us came without our families and worked hard in ironworks and shipyards.

R6:   We came to Delaware, Pennsylvania, New York, and New Jersey.

R7:   Catherine, Deborah, Rachel, and Anne

R1:   George, Charles, John, and Nathaniel

R2:   We came to the southern colonies to grow tobacco, rice, and indigo

R3:   and to make money in a new market.

R4:   We came to Maryland, Virginia, North Carolina, South Carolina, and Georgia.

R5:   Margaret, Helene, Aimee, and Abigail

R6:   Byron, Hans, Philip, and Pierre

Preamble to the Constitution
Reader's Theater *(cont.)*

All: **in order to form a more perfect union**

R7:   To solidify our nation and join together bringing our own unique characteristics

R1:   into one unified whole for the good of us all

All: **establish justice**

R2:   We had to decide what our government would do for us

R3:   and ensure that all of us would be treated fairly and equally in the eyes
of the law

R4:   No taxation without representation

All: **insure domestic tranquility**

R5:   We have had enough of war and seek peace in our nation

R6:   We stood by England in the French and Indian War

R7:   and fought against her for the right to govern ourselves

All: **provide for the common defense**

R1:   To protect all of the citizens from enemies of our nation

R2:   it is the duty of our government to protect our lives, liberty, and property

All: **promote the general welfare**

R3:   and foster the good of all the citizens

All: **and secure the blessings of liberty to ourselves and our posterity**

R4:   We will create an active partnership between the government and the people,

R5:   we the people of this new nation,

R6:   to secure safe communities to live in and raise our children

All: **do ordain and establish this Constitution for the United States of America**

R7:   The Constitutional Convention met at the State House in Philadelphia

R1:   There were 55 delegates to the Convention

R2:   Twelve of the thirteen states were represented

R3:   The Constitution was ratified on June 21, 1788.

All: **We the people of the United States, in order to form a more perfect union,
establish justice, insure domestic tranquility, provide for the common
defense, promote the general welfare, and secure the blessings of liberty
to ourselves and our posterity, do ordain and establish this Constitution
for the United States of America.**

The First Ten Amendments

Objective

√ Students will determine the meaning of text and then participate in an oral reading of public proclamations, focusing on accuracy, voice tone, and expression.

Materials

- copies of *The Bill of Rights* (page 94) for the students
- copies of *The Bill of Rights—Divided Reading* (pages 95–97) cut apart for the students
- copies of *Analyzing the Bill of Rights* (pages 98–99) for the students
- dictionaries and thesauri

Fluency Suggestions and Activities

You may want to complete the history and/or vocabulary activities on the following page before this fluency activity. An understanding of the historical context and vocabulary will help students analyze and read the piece fluently.

1. Explain that to help understand the Bill of Rights, the students will rewrite the amendments into their own words. Divide the class into nine groups and present each with a section from *The Bill of Rights—Divided Reading* (pages 95–97). (Amendments IX and X are combined.)

2. Allow students time in class to read their amendment(s) and rewrite each using current language. Provide each group with a dictionary and thesaurus to assist them in this process. Provide assistance to groups as they work to rewrite their amendments. For example, the first amendment might read:

   Congress will not make laws that establish a certain religion or prevent religious practices. Congress will not limit the freedom of the people or press to say what they want. All people will have the right to gather together in a peaceful way. People will have the right to ask the government to hear their complaints in order to solve problems.

3. Once the groups have rewritten their amendments, have them practice group readings of both the original versions and the new versions, focusing on accurate and smooth reading using appropriate expression.

4. Explain to students that when a public proclamation is recited or read (such as a reading of the Bill or Rights or reciting the Pledge of Allegiance), people use a different voice tone from regular conversation. They "announce" the words and speak with conviction and confidence.

5. Instruct the group members to practice reading both versions of their amendments as public proclamations. Finally, have each group present its amendment to the class, with a few group members reading the original version and a few reading the rewritten version.

The First Ten Amendments *(cont.)*

History Connection

Introduce the Bill of Rights and discuss its history using the information below.

When the Constitution was being written, many delegates wanted to make sure the government didn't have too much power. They kept thinking about Great Britain's power over them when they were colonists. Some of the delegates were upset by the final document because the rights of the people were not included.

By 1791, the Bill of Rights was added. The Bill of Rights is the first ten amendments to the Constitution. The Bill of Rights got its name because these first ten amendments protect the rights of all Americans.

Vocabulary Connection

Discuss unfamiliar vocabulary encountered in the text. Some possible words are listed below. After identifying the difficult words, discuss them within the context of the text.

- **abridging**—shortening something
- **redress**—to sort something out and make it right
- **infringed**—taken away
- **quartered**—given food and shelter
- **consent**—permission
- **affirmation**—to state positively
- **indictment**—when someone is charged with a crime
- **compensation**—to be given money or other goods to make up for losing something else
- **prosecutions**—the processes involved when someone is charged with a crime
- **ascertained**—figured out
- **accusation**—being blamed for doing something wrong
- **compulsory**—mandatory
- **controversy**—expressing different views
- **enumeration**—to specifically list in order
- **disparage**—to lower in position

Extension Ideas

- Encourage discussion of the amendments. Allow students to ask group members to further explain their amendments. Also, encourage them to compare the words in the original versions to the words chosen for the rewritten versions.

- Have students meet with their groups to answer the discussion questions on *Analyzing the Bill of Rights* (pages 98–99).

The Bill of Rights

Amendment I—Congress shall make no law respecting an establishment of religion, or prohibiting the free exercise thereof; or abridging the freedom of speech, or of the press; or the right of the people peaceably to assemble, and to petition the government for a redress of grievances.

Amendment II—A well regulated militia, being necessary to the security of a free state, the right of the people to keep and bear arms, shall not be infringed.

Amendment III—No soldier shall, in time of peace be quartered in any house, without the consent of the owner, nor in time of war, but in a manner to be prescribed by law.

Amendment IV—The right of the people to be secure in their persons, houses, papers, and effects, against unreasonable searches and seizures, shall not be violated, and no warrants shall issue, but upon probable cause, supported by oath or affirmation, and particularly describing the place to be searched, and the persons or things to be seized.

Amendment V—No person shall be held to answer for a capital, or otherwise infamous crime, unless on a presentment or indictment of a grand jury, except in cases arising in the land or naval forces, or in the militia, when in actual service in time of war or public danger; nor shall any person be subject for the same offense to be twice put in jeopardy of life or limb; nor shall be compelled in any criminal case to be a witness against himself, nor be deprived of life, liberty, or property, without due process of law; nor shall private property be taken for public use, without just compensation.

Amendment VI—In all criminal prosecutions, the accused shall enjoy the right to a speedy and public trial, by an impartial jury of the state and district wherein the crime shall have been committed, which district shall have been previously ascertained by law, and to be informed of the nature and cause of the accusation; to be confronted with the witnesses against him; to have compulsory process for obtaining witnesses in his favor, and to have the assistance of counsel for his defense.

Amendment VII—In suits at common law, where the value in controversy shall exceed twenty dollars, the right of trial by jury shall be preserved, and no fact tried by a jury, shall be otherwise reexamined in any court of the United States, than according to the rules of the common law.

Amendment VIII—Excessive bail shall not be required, nor excessive fines imposed, nor cruel and unusual punishments inflicted.

Amendment IX—The enumeration in the Constitution, of certain rights, shall not be construed to deny or disparage others retained by the people.

Amendment X—The powers not delegated to the United States by the Constitution, nor prohibited by it to the states, are reserved to the states respectively, or to the people.

Name _____

Bill of Rights—Divided Reading

Group 1

Amendment I—Congress shall make no law respecting an establishment of religion, or prohibiting the free exercise thereof; or abridging the freedom of speech, or of the press; or the right of the people peaceably to assemble, and to petition the government for a redress of grievances.

Rewritten version: _____

_____

_____

_____

Group 2

Amendment II—A well regulated militia, being necessary to the security of a free state, the right of the people to keep and bear arms, shall not be infringed.

Rewritten version: _____

_____

_____

_____

Group 3

Amendment III—No soldier shall, in time of peace be quartered in any house, without the consent of the owner, nor in time of war, but in a manner to be prescribed by law.

Rewritten version: _____

_____

_____

_____

Name _____

Bill of Rights—Divided Reading (cont.)

Group 4

Amendment IV—The right of the people to be secure in their persons, houses, papers, and effects, against unreasonable searches and seizures, shall not be violated, and no warrants shall issue, but upon probable cause, supported by oath or affirmation, and particularly describing the place to be searched, and the persons or things to be seized.

Rewritten version: _____

_____

_____

Group 5

Amendment V—No person shall be held to answer for a capital, or otherwise infamous crime, unless on a presentment or indictment of a grand jury, except in cases arising in the land or naval forces, or in the militia, when in actual service in time of war or public danger; nor shall any person be subject for the same offense to be twice put in jeopardy of life or limb; nor shall be compelled in any criminal case to be a witness against himself, nor be deprived of life, liberty, or property, without due process of law; nor shall private property be taken for public use, without just compensation.

Rewritten version: _____

_____

_____

Group 6

Amendment VI—In all criminal prosecutions, the accused shall enjoy the right to a speedy and public trial, by an impartial jury of the state and district wherein the crime shall have been committed, which district shall have been previously ascertained by law, and to be informed of the nature and cause of the accusation; to be confronted with the witnesses against him; to have compulsory process for obtaining witnesses in his favor, and to have the assistance of counsel for his defense.

Rewritten version: _____

_____

_____

Name _____

Bill of Rights—Divided Reading *(cont.)*

Group 7

Amendment VII—In suits at common law, where the value in controversy shall exceed twenty dollars, the right of trial by jury shall be preserved, and no fact tried by a jury, shall be otherwise reexamined in any court of the United States, than according to the rules of the common law.

Rewritten version: _____

_____

_____

_____

Group 8

Amendment VIII—Excessive bail shall not be required, nor excessive fines imposed, nor cruel and unusual punishments inflicted.

Rewritten version: _____

_____

_____

Group 9

Amendment IX—The enumeration in the Constitution, of certain rights, shall not be construed to deny or disparage others retained by the people.

Amendment X—The powers not delegated to the United States by the Constitution, nor prohibited by it to the states, are reserved to the states respectively, or to the people.

Rewritten versions: _____

_____

_____

Name _____

Analyzing the Bill of Rights

Directions: Meet with your group to discuss the questions below. You will want to have a copy of the Bill of Rights (page 94) with you as you discuss these. Turn in one copy of your group's answers written on the lines below.

1. What would life be like in our country without these rights?

   _____

   _____

   _____

2. Why do think freedom of religion was made a right to all people?

   _____

   _____

   _____

3. Why should people have the right to say what they want?

   _____

   _____

   _____

4. Why do you think colonists thought the right to bear arms was important?

   _____

   _____

   _____

5. Why do you think there is an amendment against having your home searched without probable cause?

   _____

   _____

   _____

Analyzing the Bill of Rights *(cont.)*

6. Why do you think a person can't be tried for the same crime twice?

_____

_____

_____

_____

7. Why is there a right to a speedy trial? What could happen without this?

_____

_____

_____

_____

8. Why is it important to have trials by jury?

_____

_____

_____

_____

9. What is bail and why should it not be excessive?

_____

_____

_____

_____

10. Why are some government powers given to the state? What does it mean that some powers are given to the people?

_____

_____

_____

_____

Arriving in the New World

Objective

√ Students will participate in a cooperative learning activity to enhance comprehension and improve expressive reading skills by engaging in reader's theater.

Materials

- copy of *Columbus Landing Journal Notes* (page 102) for the teacher
- copies of *Columbus Landing—Reader's Theater* (page 103) for the students
- copies of *Creating Reader's Theater* (page 104) for the students
- copies of *Analyzing the Columbus Landing Journal Notes* (page 105) for the students
- research materials such as: books, encyclopedias, Internet search engine, etc.

Fluency Suggestions and Activities

You may want to complete the history and/or vocabulary activities on the following page before this fluency activity. An understanding of the historical context and vocabulary will help students analyze and read the piece fluently.

1. Read the first few paragraphs of *Columbus Landing Journal Notes* (page 102) with expression to demonstrate how to read fluently.

2. Explain to the students that they will read the text in the form of reader's theater. Explain that this is a shared reading activity, where several students take turns reading parts of the text. Some parts of the selection are read by individual students; and some parts are read by all students.

3. Divide the students into groups of five and distribute copies of the *Columbus Landing— Reader's Theater* (page 103). Assign each student in the group a part to read. Parts are labeled R1 (for Reader 1) to R5. Draw their attention to the parts to be read by "All" students. (This is a slightly altered version of the actual text.)

4. Allow the students time in class to practice. Encourage them to focus on expression when they read as well as accuracy and reading rate.

5. Explain that it will be necessary for the audience to have more background information about Columbus in order to have a clear understanding of his journal notes. To do this, they will research and create an introduction. The introduction will be written in reader's theater format as well. Distribute copies of *Creating Reader's Theater* (page 104) to students. Instruct the students to conduct research about Columbus' journeys, what inspired him to make the journeys, and any misconceptions he might have had about the trips. To write the introduction, each group designates five parts (one for each group member). When writing the script they indicate parts with R1, R2, R3, R4, R5, and All. Encourage them to designate parts with great impact or emphasis for "All" to read.

6. After the students have practiced the reader's theater, tell them that they will be performing it for another class (or larger group of students or parents). Allow the students time to practice their introductions along with the reader's theater of Columbus' journal notes. You may want to have the students perform their reader's theaters for the class before they perform them for other audiences. Time the presentations to coincide with Columbus Day in October.

Arriving in the New World *(cont.)*

History Connection

Begin the lesson by introducing Columbus and discussing the historical information provided below. Then, read the title of the text selection and ask them to address the following questions: What do you know about Christopher Columbus? Why do you think Columbus kept a journal of his adventures? What kinds of things do you think he recorded in his journal?

Christopher Columbus was one of the finest sailors of his time. He hoped to find a shorter route to India, China, and Japan by traveling west through uncharted waters. The trip took longer than expected because Columbus did not know that Earth was as large as it is. He thought it was smaller. He did not tell the sailors the actual distance traveled each day because they would worry about being far away from home. He encouraged his men with promises of riches and fame. He kept a record of this journey in his logbook.

Vocabulary Connection

Discuss unfamiliar vocabulary encountered in the text. Some possible words are listed below. After identifying the difficult words, discuss them within the context of the text.

- **resistance**—a force that stops something from being done
- **illustrious**—someone who is considered brilliant because of the things they have achieved
- **monarch**—a king or a queen
- **proclamation**—official statement
- **unfurled**—opened
- **verdant**—when something is green in color
- **luxuriant**—fertile or fruitful
- **inhabitants**—people who live somewhere
- **trifles**—items that are not worth very much
- **forbade**—did not allow someone to do something
- **descended**—came down
- **celestial**—otherworldly, heavenly
- **astonishing**—surprising
- **affection**—feelings of love

Extension Idea

- Have students work together in their groups to gain greater understanding of Columbus and his journey to America by completing the activity sheet, *Analyzing the Columbus Landing Journal Notes* (page 105).

Columbus Landing Journal Notes

By Christopher Columbus (1492)

THIRTY-THREE days after my departure from Cadiz I reached the Indian Sea, where I discovered many islands which were thickly peopled. I took possession of these without resistance in the name of our most illustrious Monarch, by a public proclamation and with unfurled banners . . . .

All these islands are very beautiful; they are filled with a great variety of trees of immense height which retain their foliage in all seasons, I believe, for when I saw them they were as verdant and luxuriant as they usually are in Spain in the month of May. Some of them were blossoming, some bearing fruit, and all flourishing in the greatest perfection. Yet the islands are not so thickly wooded as to be impassable. The nightingale and various birds were singing in countless numbers, and that in November, the month in which I arrived there.

The inhabitants are very simple and honest, and exceedingly liberal with all they have; none of them refusing anything he may possess when he is asked for it; but on the contrary inviting us to ask them. They exhibit great love towards all others in preference to themselves: they also give objects of area value for trifles, and content themselves with very little in return. I, however, forbade that these trifles and articles of no value, such as pieces of dishes, plates, and glass, keys, and leather straps should be given to them; although if they could obtain them, they imagined themselves to be possessed of the most beautiful trinkets in the world.

On my arrival in the new world I took some Indians by force from the first island to which I came, in order that they might learn our language. These men are still travelling with me, and although they have been with us now for a long time, they continue to entertain the idea that I have descended from heaven. On our arrival at any new place they publish this, crying out immediately with a loud voice to the other Indians, "Come, come and look upon beings of a celestial race": upon which both women and men, children and adults, young men and old, when they get rid of the fear they at first entertain, will come out in throngs, crowding the roads to see us, some bringing food and others drink, with astonishing affection and kindness.

Source: *Hart, Albert Bushnell and Blanche E. Hazard.* Colonial Children.

Name _____

Columbus Landing—Reader's Theater

R1: THIRTY-THREE days after my departure from Cadiz I reached the Indian Sea, where I discovered many islands with many people.

R2: I took possession of these without resistance in the name of our king,

All: **by a public proclamation and with unfurled banners.**

R3: All these islands are very beautiful; they are filled with a great variety of tall trees, which stay healthy in all seasons,

R4: I believe, for when I saw them they were as green and full as they usually are in Spain in the month of May.

R5: Some of them were blossoming, some bearing fruit, and all growing in the greatest perfection.

R1: Yet the islands are not so thickly wooded as to be impassable. The nightingale and various birds were singing in countless numbers, even in November when I arrived there.

R2: The inhabitants are very simple and honest, and generous with all they have; none of them refusing anything he may possess when he is asked for it; but even inviting us to ask them.

R3: They exhibit great love towards all others over themselves: they also give objects of value for trifles, and are fine with very little in return.

R4: I forbade that these trifles and articles of no value, such as pieces of dishes, plates, glass, keys, and leather straps should be given to them;

R5: although if they could obtain them, they believed they held the most beautiful items in the world.

R1: On my arrival in the new world I took some Indians by force from the first island. I wanted them to learn our language.

R2: These men are still travelling with me, and although they have been with us now for a long time, they believe that I have descended

All: **from heaven.**

R3: On our arrival at any new place they tell this to everyone, crying out immediately with a loud voice to the other Indians,

All: **"Come, come and look upon beings of a celestial race"**

R4: upon which both women and men, children and adults, young men and old,

R5: when they get rid of their initial fear,

R1: will come out in throngs, crowding the roads to see us,

R2: some bringing food and others drink, with astonishing affection and kindness.

Name _____

Creating Reader's Theater

Directions: Write your introduction about Christopher Columbus as a reader's theater script below. Be sure to identify the reader (R1, R2, R3, etc.). Also, be sure to determine lines that will be read by "All." You may want to use a highlighter pen to draw attention to the lines read by all students in your group.

_____

_____

_____

_____

_____

_____

_____

_____

_____

_____

_____

_____

_____

_____

_____

_____

_____

_____

_____

Name _____

Analyzing the Columbus Landing Journal Notes

Directions: Meet in a small group to answer the questions below.

1. In his journal, Columbus writes, "I took possession of these without resistance. . . ." What does he mean by this?

   _____

   _____

2. Why do you think the native people did not resist Columbus?

   _____

   _____

3. Columbus "took possession" of some of the people he met. How do you feel about him doing this?

   _____

   _____

   _____

4. The people believed Columbus was from heaven. How would that explain their behavior toward him?

   _____

   _____

   _____

5. Some of the Indians were taught Columbus' language and then they traveled with him. Do you think this was against their will or by choice? Explain your answer.

   _____

   _____

   _____

The Explorer Columbus

Objective

√ Students will deliver paired-reading, oral presentations, performing a poem for two voices fluently with changes in tone, voice, timing, and expression.

Materials

- copy of the poem "Columbus" (page 108) for the teacher
- copies of *"Columbus"—A Poem for Two Voices* (pages 109–110) for the students
- copies of *Analyzing "Columbus"* (page 111) for the students

Fluency Suggestions and Activities

You may want to complete the history and/or vocabulary activities on the following page before this fluency activity. An understanding of the historical context and vocabulary will help students analyze and read the piece fluently.

Note: You may want to hold these presentations during October around Columbus Day.

1. Read the poem, "Columbus" (page 108), aloud for the students, modeling fluent reading, and ask them to offer their thoughts about its content. Then ask the students to address the following questions:

   - How did the mates feel about the journey at sea?
   - Why do they keep asking the Admiral what they will do?
   - Who is the Admiral?
   - Why do the mates lose hope when the Admiral does not?
   - On what does the Admiral stay focused?

2. Explain to the students that they will read and perform this poem as a poem for two voices. Explain that with this kind of reading, one person reads the words for Voice 1 and another person reads the words for Voice 2. Distribute copies of *"Columbus"—A Poem for Two Voices* (pages 109–110). Draw their attention to the way the words are divided into parts for Voice 1 and Voice 2. Voice 1 begins the reading because the first line of the poem is below that heading. The next line falls under the heading Voice 2. Some lines of the poem are read together, as they fall below both headings in the same place. These lines are also indicated in bold text.

3. Invite two students to demonstrate reading of a few lines of the poem for the class. Tell the students that this kind of poem takes practice to read fluently.

4. Divide the students into pairs and allow them time to practice reading their parts.

5. Arrange to have pairs of students present their poems for different classes.

The Explorer Columbus *(cont.)*

History Connection

Discuss the explorations of Columbus and the history behind the poem "Columbus" using the information below.

Christopher Columbus was born in 1451 in Genoa, Italy. Since no one had sailed around the world yet, no one knew the size of Earth. Columbus thought that ships could reach Asia by sailing west. This would take him over the Atlantic Ocean. Others thought that Earth was too large to sail across. Many feared a ship's crew would starve before reaching land.

Columbus tried to get money from King John of Portugal. Columbus' plan did not interest the king. Columbus then asked King Ferdinand and Queen Isabella of Spain for help. He told them that this trip could make Spain rich. He said he would help convert people to Christianity. The king and queen made him wait six long years while Spain fought a war. When the war was over, they gave him three ships, supplies, and a crew.

Vocabulary Connection

Discuss unfamiliar vocabulary encountered in the text. Some possible words are listed below. After identifying the difficult words, discuss them within the context of the text.

- **Azores**—islands off the coast of Portugal
- **mutinous**—in a state of rebellion
- **ghastly**—horribly
- **wan**—pale and sick
- **swarthy**—dark coloring in someone's skin
- **naught**—nothing
- **blanched**—very pale and colorless
- **dread**—great fear
- **unfurled**—opened

Extension Ideas

- Assist students with increasing their comprehension of the poem. Have them work together in small groups to analyze the poem using the activity sheet, *Analyzing "Columbus"* (page 111). Encourage them to refer to the poem as they discuss it and answer the questions.
- Have groups of students teach other classes how to read a poem for two voices. They distribute copies of *"Columbus"—A Poem for Two Voices* to the students in the class. Your group of students should read Voice 1 and the students in the assigned class read Voice 2. Have them practice the reading several times to increase fluency.

Columbus

By Joaquin Miller

BEHIND him lay the gray Azores,
  Behind the Gates of Hercules;
Before him not the ghost of shores,
  Before him only shoreless seas.
The good mate said: "Now must we pray,
  For lo! the very stars are gone.
Brave Admiral, speak, what shall I say?"
  "Why, say, 'Sail on! sail on! and on!'"

"My men grow mutinous day by day;
  My men grow ghastly wan and weak."
The stout mate thought of home; a spray
  Of salt wave washed his swarthy cheek.
"What shall I say, brave Admiral, say,
  If we sight naught but seas at dawn?"
"Why, you shall say at break of day,
  'Sail on! sail on! sail on! and on!'"

They sailed and sailed, as winds might blow,
  Until at last the blanched mate said:
"Why, now not even God would know
  Should I and all my men fall dead.
These very winds forget their way,
  For God from these dread seas is gone.
Now speak, brave Admiral, speak and say"—
  He said: "Sail on! sail on! and on!"

They sailed. They sailed. Then spake the mate:
  "This mad sea shows his teeth to-night.
He curls his lip, he lies in wait,
  With lifted teeth, as if to bite!
Brave Admiral, say but one good word:
  What shall we do when hope is gone?"
The words leapt like a leaping sword:
  "Sail on! sail on! sail on! and on!"

Then, pale and worn, he kept his deck,
  And peered through darkness. Ah, that night
Of all dark nights! And then a speck—
  A light! A light! A light! A light!
It grew, a starlit flag unfurled!
  It grew to be Time's burst of dawn.
He gained a world; he gave that world
  Its grandest lesson: "On! sail on!"

Name _____

"Columbus"—A Poem for Two Voices

Voice 1

BEHIND him lay the gray Azores,

Before him not the ghost of shores,

The good mate said: "Now must we pray,

Brave Admiral, speak, what shall I say?"

"Why, say, 'Sail on! sail on! and on!'"

My men grow ghastly wan and weak."

Of salt wave washed his swarthy cheek.

If we sight naught but seas at dawn?"

'Sail on! sail on! sail on! and on!'"

They sailed and sailed, as winds might blow,

"Why, now not even God would know

These very winds forget their way,

Now speak, brave Admiral, speak and say"—

He said: "Sail on! sail on! and on!"

Voice 2

Behind the Gates of Hercules;

Before him only shoreless seas.

For lo! the very stars are gone.

"Why, say, 'Sail on! sail on! and on!'"
"My men grow mutinous day by day;

The stout mate thought of home; a spray

"What shall I say, brave Admiral, say,

"Why, you shall say at break of day,

'Sail on! sail on! sail on! and on!'"

Until at last the blanched mate said:

Should I and all my men fall dead.

For God from these dread seas is gone.

He said: "Sail on! sail on! and on!"

"Columbus"—A Poem for Two Voices (cont.)

Voice 1	Voice 2
They sailed. They sailed. Then spake the mate:	
	"This mad sea shows his teeth to-night.
He curls his lip, he lies in wait,	
	With lifted teeth, as if to bite!
Brave Admiral, say but one good word:	
	What shall we do when hope is gone?"
The words leapt like a leaping sword:	
"Sail on! sail on! sail on! and on!"	**"Sail on! sail on! sail on! and on!"**
	Then, pale and worn, he kept his deck,
And peered through darkness. Ah, that night	
	Of all dark nights! And then a speck—
A light! A light! A light! A light!	**A light! A light! A light! A light!**
It grew, a starlit flag unfurled!	
	It grew to be Time's burst of dawn.
He gained a world; he gave that world	
	Its grandest lesson:
"On! sail on!"	**"On! sail on!"**

Name _____

Analyzing "Columbus"

Directions: Work with a group of students to analyze Joaquin Miller's poem "Columbus." Answer the questions below.

1. What words do the mates say that indicate that they are afraid?

   _____

   _____

   _____

   _____

2. Why are the men losing hope?

   _____

   _____

   _____

3. *Personification* is the use of human terms to describe inanimate objects. How is personification used in this poem to describe the sea?

   _____

   _____

   _____

   _____

4. What happens in the poem that gives the mate hope?

   _____

   _____

   _____

   _____

   _____

Pocahontas of the Powhatan Tribe

Objective

√ Students will read aloud fluently and accurately with changes in tone, voice, timing, and expression using cumulative choral reading.

Materials

- copies of the poem "The Ballad of Pocahontas" (page 114) for the students
- optional: roll of light brown paper, paint, fabric, yarn, wood, and feathers for the Extension Idea

Fluency Suggestions and Activities

You may want to complete the history and/or vocabulary activities on the following page before this fluency activity. An understanding of the historical context and vocabulary will help students analyze and read the piece fluently.

1. Give each student a copy of "The Ballad of Pocahontas" (page 114). Read it aloud modeling fluent reading.

2. Next, read the poem slowly, as a choral reading with the entire class. After each stanza, stop and look for clues in the text that tell you how to read it (e.g., commas, exclamation marks, periods, repetition).

3. Then, explain what a cumulative choral reading is to the class. Tell them that two students will start reading the poem by themselves. Then, after two lines, two more students will join them. The students will continue reading the poem as more and more students join in every two lines.

4. To begin, you will need to assign parts to the students and give them a chance to practice. There are 28 lines in the poem. So, depending on how many students you have, you will need to assign one to four students to every two lines. It is suggested that you assign your stronger readers to the earlier parts because they will have to read more of the poem.

5. Give students plenty of time to practice their parts. Invite another class or staff members into the classroom for your final performance. (The librarian and music teacher in your school might enjoy seeing this performance.)

Pocahontas of the Powhatan Tribe *(cont.)*

History Connection

Introduce Pocahontas and the Powhatan Indians using the information provided below.

Around 1595, a young Indian girl was born. Her name was Matoaka. This means "Little Snow Feather." Her father decided to call her Pocahontas. Pocahontas means "playful one." She had lots of energy and enjoyed playing outdoors. Her family lived in the Chesapeake Bay region.

Pocahontas first saw British settlers in 1607. They lived in a colony called Fort James. Later, the fort's name was changed to Jamestown. Pocahontas was a regular visitor to Jamestown. She talked often with a man named John Smith. He wanted to learn from the Indians. The settlers were not very good at growing crops. Smith visited the Indian villages to trade for food.

Vocabulary Connection

Discuss unfamiliar vocabulary encountered in the text. Some possible words are listed below. After identifying the difficult words, discuss them within the context of the text.

- **scores**—large numbers
- **brief**—short
- **defend**—fight for something and keep it safe
- **palefaced**—when someone's face has light-colored skin, white men
- **ransom**—when a kidnapper asks for money to release a prisoner

Extension Idea

- Students can create a time line of events in the life of Pocahontas. Use a roll of light brown paper for the time line so it can be displayed along a wall or hung from the ceiling in the classroom. First, decide which events will be depicted on the time line. Next, draw or paint a time line where dates and events will be written. The time line helps students to comprehend the sequence of events. Keep enough space along the time line between events for pictures with captions. Pictures can be drawn or painted directly on the brown paper or illustrations can be completed on another paper and glued along the time line. Use bits of fabric, yarn, wood, feathers, or any other materials that will bring some interest and texture to the pictures. Ask students to write a brief caption for each illustration.

The Ballad of Pocahontas

The Indians of Virginia's tribes
Had known some very peaceful times—
Before the English sailing ships
Arrived with scores of colonists.

John Smith went to look around—
A band of warriors took him, bound
To stand before the Indian chief,
He hoped his visit would be brief.

Pocahontas was there to defend
The white man was her newest friend.
She felt that there would be no danger
Living near the palefaced stranger.

The winter brought cold winds and snow,
The settlers had nowhere to go.
When they were starving and afraid
The Indians came with corn to trade.

Pocahontas and the white men knew
Their friendship was not really true.
They took her captive on a boat
And sent the chief a ransom note.

Her father left her many days
So she learned the English ways.
When she gave John Rolfe her hand,
They visited his native land.

There she met John Smith again,
The King and Queen became her friends.
She thought about how much she'd done
To help two nations live as one.

Pocahontas and John Rolfe

Objective

√ Students will read passages fluently and accurately within a paired-reading activity.

Materials

• copies of *The Wedding of Pocahontas* (page 117) for the students

Fluency Suggestions and Activities

You may want to complete the history and/or vocabulary activities on the following page before this fluency activity. An understanding of the historical context and vocabulary will help students analyze and read the piece fluently.

1. Distribute and introduce *The Wedding of Pocahontas* (page 117). Model an expressive reading of the text.

2. Divide the students into predetermined reading pairs. Try to pair a low reader (partner A), with a high reader (partner B). Have the students read the selection within their pairs. The "B" partners should read alone first. These are the stronger students and by reading first, they are modeling fluent reading of the passage.

3. The "A" partners are more likely going to have difficulty reading the passage fluently. They should follow along on a printed copy of the text while listening to the "B" partner read. Then, the two students can read the passage together. Finally, the "A" partner can read the selection independently with help from the fluent reader.

4. After several opportunities to read the text, invite students who wish to read aloud to do so. This can be done individually, in pairs, or in small groups. They can read the whole text or just one section that they especially enjoyed.

Pocahontas and John Rolfe (cont.)

History Connection

Give the students background information on the text from the information provided below.

The kidnapping of Pocahontas changed her life. As the newly baptised Rebecca, she fell in love with a man named John Rolfe. Her captors allowed her to see her father once more. She told him she was in love with Rolfe. Chief Powhatan gave his blessing. She got married on April 5, 1614.

Jamestown was not doing well. In 1616, the governor thought of a way to raise some money. He wanted to take some Indians to England. The Indians would help convince others to settle in the New World. John Rolfe, Rebecca, and their one-year-old son, Thomas, were part of this group. Rebecca even got to meet King James I.

Vocabulary Connection

Discuss unfamiliar vocabulary encountered in the text. Some possible words are listed below. After identifying the difficult words, discuss them within the context of the text.

- **provisions**—food and supplies
- **respite**—rest
- **harvest**—the time when crops are picked
- **weir**—a fence that is build in a river to catch fish
- **conferring**—meeting and discussing
- **consent**—permission
- **solemnized**—celebrated
- **thrive**—grow well
- **apace**—quickly

Extension Ideas

- Have each student write a journal entry or letter about the wedding as if he or she was a member of Powhatan's tribe. Ask the student to use the information they have acquired from reading the text and any other information about the wedding that they can access from resource materials. Information in the letter might include descriptions of the clothing, setting, foods, ceremony, those in attendance, and so on. Encourage creativity along with historical accuracy.

- Discuss the meaning of the selection for comprehension. Note any words that differ in use from our speaking vocabulary of today, for example: departed, gentleman of approved behavior and honest carriage, thereto, thrive apace, and so on. Ask students about the meanings of the words and phrases and give examples of how we would say the same thing using contemporary language.

The Wedding of Pocahontas

By Raphe Hamor

It was then April and the time of year called us to our business at home, to prepare ground and to plant corn for our winter's provisions; so we departed upon these terms, giving the Indians respite till harvest, to decide what was best for them to do. We told them clearly that if a final agreement were not made between us before that time, we should return again and destroy or take away all their corn, burn all the houses upon that river, leave not a fishing weir standing nor a canoe in any creek thereabouts, and kill as many of them as we could.

Long before this time, a gentleman of approved behavior and honest carriage, Master John Rolfe fell in love with Pocahontas and she with him. Of this fact I made Sir Thomas Dale aware by a letter from Master John Rolfe, even while we were conferring and making conditions with Powhatan's men. In the letter Rolfe begged Dale's advice and assistance in his love, if it seemed to him for the good of the Plantation. Pocahontas herself told her brothers about it. Sir Thomas Dale's approval of the match was the only reason why he was so mild amongst Powhatan's people. Otherwise he would not have departed from their river, without other conditions.

The rumor of this intended marriage soon came to Powhatan's knowledge and was acceptable to him, as appeared by his sudden consent thereto. Some ten days after he sent an old uncle of hers, named Opachisco, to give her away in the church as his deputy, and two of his sons to see the marriage solemnized. This was done about the fifth of April, and ever since then we have had friendly relations not only with Powhatan himself, but also with his subjects round about us; so that now I see no reason why the colony should not thrive apace.

Source: *Hart, Albert Bushnell with Blanche E. Hazard.* Colonial Children.

From Africa to America

Objective

√ Students will read passages fluently and accurately within an oral reading activity, focusing on correct phrasing.

Materials

- copies of the poem "On Being Brought from Africa to America" (page 120) for the students
- copies of *Analyzing "On Being Brought from Africa to America"* (page 121) for the students
- optional: copies of the excerpt of the poem "On the Death of the Rev. Mr. George Whitefield" (page 122)

Fluency Suggestions and Activities

You may want to complete the history and/or vocabulary activities on the following page before this fluency activity. An understanding of the historical context and vocabulary will help students analyze and read the piece fluently.

Note: In Massachusetts, Phillis Wheatley Day is celebrated on February 1. You may want to join that state in celebration and have students give a presentation at a school assembly. You could also have a daily poetry reading over the school's loud speaker during the celebration week.

1. Begin the lesson by dividing the students into small groups. Provide each student with a copy of *Analyzing "On Being Brought from Africa to America"* (page 121). Instruct each group to discuss and answer only questions one through three. Then gather the class together to discuss their responses to the questions.

2. Distribute copies of the poem "On Being Brought from Africa to America" (page 120) to students. Read the poem aloud, demonstrating fluency. Read the poem again, and draw students' attention to the phrasing used as you read. Read the first line in a choppy, word-by-word manner. Then read it fluently. Ask the students to compare the two readings. Explain that proper phrasing makes poetry easier to understand.

3. Have students complete the remainder of questions from page 121 in their groups and then discuss the poems as a class.

4. Have students work in pairs to practice reading the poem, focusing on correct phrasing. When students have had the opportunity to practice reading the poem several times and on a few different occasions, ask them to recite the poem to classmates or other students in the school.

From Africa to America *(cont.)*

History Connection

Discuss Phillis Wheatley's journey to America and what her life might have been like. Ask them how they would have felt if put in the same situation. Present the historical information provided below. After reading the poem, ask the students to address the following questions: What does "Pagan Land" mean? Why does she say *mercy* brought her out of Africa? What did her soul understand that it didn't understand before? She refers to her skin color as "diabolic die." Any ideas why? She refers to Cain in the poem. Who was he?

Phillis Wheatley was born in western Africa around 1753. When she was seven years old, she was kidnapped. She was taken on a boat to Boston, Massachusetts. Then, she was sold as a slave. A wealthy Boston man bought Phillis. His name was John Wheatley. He wanted Phillis to be a servant for his wife, Susannah. John and Susannah named Phillis after the slave ship that brought her to the colonies. Her last name became Wheatley because they owned her.

Vocabulary Connection

Discuss unfamiliar vocabulary encountered in the text. Some possible words are listed below. After identifying the difficult words, discuss them within the context of the text.

- **'twas**—it was
- **mercy**—compassion
- **pagan**—someone or something that is not religious
- **benighted**—not very well educated
- **redemption**—freeing from any consequences of sin
- **sable**—when something is black in color
- **scornful**—to dislike something
- **diabolic**—when something is related to the devil
- **Cain**—a character from the Bible
- **refin'd**—refined, when something is changed to make it better

Extension Ideas

- Challenge students to read another Phillis Wheatley poem entitled "On the Death of the Rev. Mr. George Whitefield" (page 122). Explain that this poem was written about a minister during the Great Awakening.
- Challenge your students to research the Great Awakening and share their findings with the class.

On Being Brought from Africa to America

By Phillis Wheatley

'TWAS mercy brought me from my Pagan land,

Taught my benighted soul to understand

That there's a God, that there's a Saviour too:

Once I redemption neither fought now knew,

Some view our sable race with scornful eye,

"Their colour is a diabolic die."

Remember, Christians, Negroes, black as Cain,

May be refin'd, and join th' angelic train.

Name _____

Analyzing "On Being Brought from Africa to America"

Directions: Before reading the poem, answer questions one through three. After reading the poem, work with your group to answer the remaining questions.

1. Phillis Wheatley was taken from her home in Africa and brought to America at the age of 7. How do you think she felt about this experience and her new life of slavery?

   _____

   _____

2. What do you suppose her life was like as a child in America?

   _____

   _____

3. How do you think she was treated by her owners?

   _____

   _____

   _____

4. Does she sound grateful or resentful about being brought to America?

   _____

   _____

   _____

5. Summarize the message of the poem on the lines below.

   _____

   _____

   _____

   _____

   _____

   _____

   _____

   _____

   _____

   _____

Excerpt from "On the Death of the Rev. Mr. George Whitefield"

By Phillis Wheatley in 1770

Great Countess, we Americans revere

Thy name, and mingle in thy grief sincere;

New England deeply feels, the Orphans mourn,

Their more than father will no more return.

But, though arrested by the hand of death,

Whitefield no more exerts his lab'ring breath,

Yet let us view him in th' eternal skies,

Let ev'ry heart to this bright vision rise;

While the tomb safe retains its sacred trust,

Till life divine re-animates his dust.

Earl of Dartmouth

Objective

√ Students will participate in paired-reading experiences, focusing on smooth reading, accuracy, reading rate, and expression.

Materials

- copies of the excerpt of the poem "To the Right Honourable William, Earl of Dartmouth, His Majesty's Principal Secretary of State for North-America, &c." (page 125) for the students
- copies of the *Rewritten Version of Wheatley's Poem* (page 126) for the students
- copies of *Assessing Fluency* (page 127) for parent volunteers
- copies of *Fluency Chart* (page 128) for parent volunteers
- optional: copies of the poem "A Farewel to America. To Mrs. S. W." (page 129) for the students

Fluency Suggestions and Activities

You may want to complete the history and/or vocabulary activities on the following page before this fluency activity. An understanding of the historical context and vocabulary will help students analyze and read the piece fluently.

Note: In preparation for the lesson, enlist the help of several parent volunteers as reading partners and evaluators.

1. Explain to students that they will be reading one of Phillis Wheatley's poems. (If you are planning to have a Phillis Wheatley celebration, explain that the poems in this lesson will be read publicly during that time.) Read aloud the poem, "To the Right Honourable William, Earl of Dartmouth, His Majesty's Principal Secretary of State for North-America, &c." (page 125), modeling fluency.

2. Explain that this is merely an excerpt from a much longer poem. It is the only time that Wheatley mentions slavery in poetry. Because the excerpt uses some challenging terms and vocabulary, explain that their reading will come from a rewritten, simplified version of the poem excerpt. Read this version aloud to the students and discuss with them the meaning of the words and the message Wheatley was likely trying to communicate.

3. Distribute copies of the simplified version (page 126) and allow students time in class to practice reading it. Encourage them to focus on reading smoothly, accurately, quickly, and with expression.

4. Enlist the help of parent volunteers to complete a paired reading of the poem excerpt. Provide each volunteer with copies of the pages, *Assessing Fluency* (page 127) and *Fluency Chart* (page 128). The first page describes the elements of fluency and explains how to complete the fluency chart.

5. When reading together, parent and student should first read the text aloud together a few times. Encourage the parent to offer praise and suggestions as needed. The student then reads the text independently as the volunteer listens for the elements of fluency. Encourage the volunteer not to complete the fluency chart until after the paired-reading experience has ended, in order not to distract the student.

Earl of Dartmouth (cont.)

History Connection

Introduce Phillis Wheatley using the information provided below. Then, ask the following questions: What do we know about Phillis Wheatley? Where was she born? How did she come to America? How did she feel about coming to America?

The life of a slave was never easy. But, Phillis was luckier than most slaves. First of all, she lived in New England. The slaves in the North were usually treated better than slaves in the South. The Wheatleys were kind to Phillis. They knew that she was special and helped her to learn. Phillis once wrote that Mrs. Wheatley treated her "more like a child than her servant."

Phillis was 14 when her first poem was published. She used poetry like a diary. She wrote about how she was feeling and what she was thinking. This was unusual for colonial poets. Most colonial poets did not share a lot of emotions in their poems.

Vocabulary Connection

Discuss unfamiliar vocabulary encountered in the text. Some possible words are listed below. After identifying the difficult words, discuss them within the context of the text.

- **peruse**—look something over
- **whence**—where
- **pangs**—bad feelings inside
- **excruciating**—very painful
- **molest**—to annoy or disturb
- **labour**—labor, to feel upset
- **seiz'd**—seized, to take something
- **belov'd**—beloved, when something is loved very much
- **tyrannic**—being completely ruled by one person
- **sway**—when something or someone controls what you do

Extension Ideas

- Challenge students to read another Phillis Wheatley poem entitled "A Farewel to America. To Mrs. S. W." (page 129). Explain that S.W. stands for Susannah Wheatley, who was Phillis Wheatley's owner while in slavery. Phillis Wheatley wrote this poem about her after her death.
- Encourage students to conduct research about slavery and share their findings with the class.

To the Right Honourable William, Earl of Dartmouth, His Majesty's Principal Secretary of State for North-America, &c.

By Phillis Wheatley

Should you, my lord, while you peruse my song,

Wonder from whence my love of Freedom sprung,

Whence flow these wishes for the common good,

By feeling hearts alone best understood,

I, young in life, by seeming cruel fate

Was snatch'd from Afric's fancy'd happy seat:

What pangs excruciating must molest,

What sorrows labour in my parent's breast?

Steel'd was that soul and by no misery mov'd

That from a father seiz'd his babe belov'd:

Such, such my case. And can I then but pray

Others may never feel tyrannic sway?

Rewritten Version of Wheatley's Poem

Earl of Dartmouth

Should you, my lord, while you read through my song,

Wonder from where my love of Freedom sprung,

Where flow these wishes for the common good,

By feeling hearts alone best understood,

I, young in life, by seeming cruel fate

Was snatched from Africa's happy seat:

What terrible pangs must attack,

What sorrows hurt my parent's heart?

Hardened was that soul and by no misery moved

That from a father took his beloved child:

Such, such my case. And can I then but pray

Others may never feel tyrannic sway?

Assessing Fluency

Directions: Use the information below to assist you in completing the fluency evaluation on page 128.

Passage: On these lines, record the passage that the student read.

Smooth Reading: Listen as the student reads the passage. Pay attention to the manner in which he or she reads.

- Does he or she hesitate between words?
- Does the reading sound "choppy"?
- Does the student have a consistent pace when reading?

Reading Rates: The goal of fluency is not to read as quickly as possible, but rather to read at a comfortable pace. Listen as the student reads the passage.

- Does the student read at a rate that is pleasant to listen to and easy to comprehend?

Accuracy: As the student reads, pay attention to the number of mistakes made. The student would receive a positive comment if he or she is able to read with 80–90% accuracy.

Expression: Part of fluent reading involves the ability to read with expression. This might involve varying the tone of voice when reading. This might also involve varying the sound of voice when different characters speak. As the student reads, consider the following questions:

- Does he or she read in monotone?
- Does he or she vary tone of voice?
- Does he or she vary voice when reading dialogue?

Student's Comments: This portion of the chart is important to complete because it encourages self-evaluation. After the student reads the passage, ask him or her the questions below and record pertinent responses.

- How do you feel about the way you read the passage?
- Was the passage difficult for you?
- Was your reading choppy or smooth?
- Did you read slowly or at a quick pace?
- Did you make many mistakes?
- How do you feel about your use of expression?

Name _____

Fluency Chart

Passage: _____

Smooth Reading: _____

_____

Reading Rates: _____

_____

Accuracy: _____

_____

Expression: _____

_____

Student's Comments: _____

_____

_____

Passage: _____

Smooth Reading: _____

_____

Reading Rates: _____

_____

Accuracy: _____

_____

Expression: _____

_____

Student's Comments: _____

_____

_____

A Farewel to America. To Mrs. S. W.

By Phillis Wheatley, Boston, May 7, 1773.

ADIEU, New-England's smiling meads,
　Adieu, the flow'ry plain:
I leave thine op'ning charms, O spring,
　And tempt the roaring main.

In vain for me the flow'rets rise,
　And boast their gaudy pride,
While here beneath the northern skies
　I mourn for health deny'd.

Celestial maid of rosy hue,
　O let me feel thy reign!
I languish till thy face I view,
　Thy vanish'd joys regain.

Susanna mourns, nor can I bear
　To see the crystal show'r,
Or mark the tender falling tear
　At sad departure's hour;

Not unregarding can I see
　Her soul with grief opprest:
But let no sighs, no groans for me,
　Steal from her pensive breast.

The Boston Massacre

Objective

√ Students will participate in cooperative learning and improve expressive reading skills by engaging in reader's theater.

Materials

- copy of *Statement for the Defense* (page 132) for the teacher
- copies of *Statement for the Defense—Reader's Theater* (pages 133–135) for the students
- highlighters
- video recorder and videotape

Fluency Suggestions and Activities

You may want to complete the history and/or vocabulary activities on the following page before this fluency activity. An understanding of the historical context and vocabulary will help students analyze and read the piece fluently.

1. Read the text of *Statement for the Defense* (page 132) aloud to the students.

2. Explain to the students that reader's theater is a shared reading activity, where several students take turns reading parts of text. Some parts of the selection are read by individual students; some parts are read by all students. Divide the students into groups of five and distribute copies of the *Statement for the Defense—Reader's Theater* (pages 133–135). Assign each student in the group a part to read. Parts are labeled R1 (for Reader 1) to R5. Draw their attention to the parts to be read by "All" students.

3. Instruct each student to use a highlighter to mark his or her parts to read in the selection. Allow students time in class to practice reading their parts.

4. Tell the students that they will have the chance to perform their reader's theater for another class. Encourage students to think about and practice how they will use hand motions and facial expressions as they read their parts.

5. Arrange to have each group present their reader's theater to a different class. Before the presentations, remind the students that they want to get the audience to experience the content of the text as if they were actually there. Make a video recording of the performances.

6. Try to find pen pals from Massachusetts, John Adams's home state. Have the students find all they can about John and Abigail Adams from their pen pals. Send the videotape to the pen pal class.

The Boston Massacre (cont.)

History Connection

Discuss the history of the Boston Massacre using the information provided below. Draw their attention to the fact that the text for this lesson was a speech by John Adams during the Boston Massacre trial. As they practice, have them consider the following questions: What kind of expression would be heard in his voice as he speaks to a judge and jury? Would his voice sound happy, concerned, angry, or forceful?

The leaders in Great Britain sent 4,000 soldiers to Boston. That meant there was one redcoat for every three colonists in town. The colonists were mean to the soldiers. They called the soldiers names and threw things at them. On March 5, 1770, a colonist got into a fight with a British guard. It started as a little thing, but then more and more people joined in the fight. The townspeople began pushing and shoving. They threw rocks and ice at the soldier. Soon eight more soldiers came to help him.

The soldiers were scared by the noisy crowd. They got nervous. When somebody yelled, "Fire!" the soldiers shot into the crowd. Five colonists were killed. The angry people called this the Boston Massacre. The soldiers were put on trial for murder. John Adams acted as their lawyer and won the case. The soldiers were found not guilty.

Vocabulary Connection

Discuss unfamiliar vocabulary encountered in the text. Some possible words are listed below. After identifying the difficult words, discuss them within the context of the text.

- **shavers**—people who get money by tricking others
- **motley rabble**—a disorganized group of people from different backgrounds
- **jack tarrs**—sailors
- **dominions**—countries that have the British king or queen as their leader
- **wretched**—poor
- **conservators**—people with the job of looking after something
- **inclinations**—personal opinions
- **provocation**—to deliberately anger something or someone
- **manslaughter**—to accidentally kill someone
- **eradicated**—erased
- **candour**—candor, fairness

Extension Idea

- Instruct groups of students to rewrite the *Statement for the Defense* (page 132) using more familiar language. Ask them to think about their understanding of Adam's speech when put in more common terms.

Statement for the Defense

A Speech by John Adams at the Boston Massacre Trial

We have been entertained with a great variety of phrases, to avoid calling this sort of people a mob. Some call them shavers, some call them geniuses. The plain English is gentlemen, most probably a motley rabble of saucy boys, negroes and mulattoes, Irish teagues and outlandish jack tarrs. And why we should scruple to call such a set of people a mob, I can't conceive, unless the name is too respectable for them: The sun is not about to stand still or go out, nor the rivers to dry up because there was a mob in Boston on the 5th of March that attacked a party of soldiers. Such things are not new in the world, nor in the British dominions, though they are comparatively, rareties and novelties in this town. Carr a native of Ireland had often been concerned in such attacks, and indeed, from the nature of things, soldiers quartered in a populous town, will always occasion two mobs, where they prevent one. They are wretched conservators of the peace!

I will enlarge no more on the evidence, but submit it to you. Facts are stubborn things; and whatever may be our wishes, our inclinations, or the dictates of our passions, they cannot alter the state of facts and evidence: nor is the law less stable than the fact; if an assault was made to endanger their lives, the law is clear, they had a right to kill in their own defence; if it was not so severe as to endanger their lives, yet if they were assaulted at all, struck and abused by blows of any sort, by snow-balls, oyster-shells, cinders, clubs, or sticks of any kind; this was a provocation, for which the law reduces the offence of killing, down to manslaughter, in consideration of those passions in our nature, which cannot be eradicated. To your candour and justice I submit the prisoners and their cause.

Courtesy of Boston Massacre Historical Society

Name _____

Statement for the Defense— Reader's Theater

R1:   Boston, Massachusetts, 1768.

R2:   Tax collectors are sent from Britain to collect money from the colonists.

R3:   But the colonists don't want them there and the tax collectors fear for their safety.

R4:   The tax collectors demand protection from the military.

R5:   The commander in chief of the British Army in America sends thousands of soldiers to Boston to protect them.

R1:   Thousands of soldiers?

All: That's an outrage!

R2:   The people of the town don't want them here.

All: They're here to make trouble! They'll take away our jobs!

R3:   The townspeople become upset.

R4:   Fights break out.

R5:   Boston, Massachusetts—March 5, 1770.

R1:   A British soldier is standing guard.

R2:   A crowd of men begin to bother the soldier.

R3:   A fight breaks out.

R4:   The townspeople throw sticks,

R5:   snowballs,

R1:   rocks.

R2:   Shots are fired.

All: Five townspeople die that day.

R3:   The British captain and eight of his soldiers are put on trial for deaths of the men.

Statement for the Defense— Reader's Theater (cont.)

R4:   John Adams

R5:   lawyer,

R1:   patriot,

R2:   representative to the Continental Congress,

R3:   signer of the Declaration of Independence,

R4:   first vice president, and second president

All: of the United States of America.

R5:   John Adams decides to defend the soldiers and help them get a fair trial.

R1:   The following are his closing arguments at the soldiers' trial.

R2:   We have been entertained with a great variety of phrases, to avoid calling this sort of people a mob.

R3:   Some call them tricksters, some call them geniuses.

R4:   The plain English is gentlemen,

R5:   most probably a mixed rabble of saucy boys,

R1:   negroes and mulattoes,

R2:   Irish teagues

R3:   and outlandish sailors.

R4:   And why we should call such a set of people a mob,

All: I can't conceive,

R5:   unless the name is too respectable for them:

R1:   The sun is not about to stand still or go out,

R2:   nor the rivers to dry up because there was a mob in Boston on the 5th of March that attacked a party of soldiers.

All: Such things are not new in the world,

R3:   nor in the British countries, though they are comparatively, rareties and novelties in this town.

Statement for the Defense— Reader's Theater (cont.)

R4: Carr a native of Ireland had often been concerned in such attacks,

R5: and indeed, from the nature of things,

R1: soldiers quartered in a populous town, will always occasion two mobs, where they prevent one.

All: They are poor keepers of the peace!

R2: I will enlarge no more on the evidence, but submit it to you.

All: Facts are stubborn things;

R3: and whatever may be our wishes, our personal opinions, or the dictates of our passions,

All: they cannot alter the state of facts and evidence:

R4: nor is the law less stable than the fact;

R5: if an assault was made to endanger their lives,

All: the law is clear,

R1: they had a right to kill in their own defense;

R2: if it was not so severe as to endanger their lives, yet if they were assaulted at all,

R3: struck and abused by blows of any sort,

R4: by snow-balls,

R5: oyster-shells,

R1: cinders,

R2: clubs, or sticks of any kind;

R3: this was a provocation, for which the law reduces the offense of killing,

R4: down to manslaughter,

R5: in consideration of those passions in our nature, which cannot be erased.

All: To your fairness and justice I submit the prisoners and their cause.

Remember the Ladies

Objective

√ Students will participate in cooperative learning and improve expressive reading skills by engaging in reader's theater.

Materials

- copy of *Remember the Ladies Letters* (page 138) for the teacher
- copies of *Remember the Ladies Letters—Reader's Theater* (pages 139–140) for the students
- highlighters

Fluency Suggestions and Activities

You may want to complete the history and/or vocabulary activities on the following page before this fluency activity. An understanding of the historical context and vocabulary will help students analyze and read the piece fluently.

1. Read the two letters included on *Remember the Ladies Letters* (page 138) to the students modeling good reading fluency.

2. Explain to the students that reader's theater is a shared reading activity, where several students take turns reading parts of text. Some parts of the selection are read by individual students; some parts are read by all students. Then, explain that they will have the opportunity to read John and Abigail Adams's letters as a reader's theater. Explain that for this particular reader's theater the boys and the girls will read separate sections. Girls will read the section, "Abigail Adams to John Adams," and the boys will respond with the section, "John Adams to Abigail Adams."

3. Divide the students into groups of four (two boys and two girls) and distribute copies of the *Remember the Ladies—Reader's Theater* (pages 139–140). Ask students to assign parts to read. Parts are labeled R1 and R2 for Reader 1 and Reader 2. Instruct each student to use a highlighter to mark his or her parts to read in the selection. Allow students time in class to practice reading their parts.

4. Encourage the students to use expression as Abigail and John Adams might have used if they had been speaking these words aloud to one another.

5. As students prepare for their reader's theater performances, ask them to plan simple costumes to wear.

6. Time this lesson to coincide with Mother's Day or Women's History Month in March. Have the students create invitations for their mothers, inviting them to come to class to see their reader's theater presentations.

Remember the Ladies (cont.)

History Connection

Read aloud the excerpt from John and Abigail Adams's "Remember the Ladies" letters and discuss the history of the time using the information below.

Abigail Adams wrote many letters to her husband John when he was in the Continental Congresses. Her letters to him were filled with love. She also asked him many questions. She wanted to know all about what he was doing. Sometimes, Abigail gave John ideas for the new laws he was writing. In one famous letter she told him to "Remember the Ladies." She believed that the new country should have fair laws for women. She wanted women to have more power over their lives. Abigail was one of the first people to talk about such an idea.

Vocabulary Connection

Discuss unfamiliar vocabulary encountered in the text. Some possible words are listed below. After identifying the difficult words, discuss them within the context of the text.

- **tyrants**—rulers who believe in absolute control by one person
- **rebelion**—rebellion, when people speak or act out against authority
- **tyrannical**—something that is like a tyrant
- **dispute**—argument
- **impunity**—freedom from punishment
- **abhor**—dislike or hate
- **apprentices**—people who are learning a job
- **turbulent**—upset or not calm
- **discontented**—unhappy
- **repeal**—call something back
- **obliged**—forced to do something
- **despotism**—to be ruled by one person
- **monarchy**—when one person (usually a king or queen) rules and has all the power
- **aristocracy**—government where only certain people (usually the rich) make decisions
- **oligarchy**—government where only a few people make decisions (usually to benefit themselves)
- **ochlocracy**—to be ruled by a mob

Extension Idea

- Discuss the meaning of "Remember the Ladies" and analyze what Abigail and John Adams are communicating to one another in their letters. Instruct each student to rewrite a section of the text reflecting his or her interpretations of it.

Remember the Ladies Letters

Abigail Adams to John Adams

March 31, 1776

I long to hear that you have declared an independancy—and by the way in the new Code of Laws which I suppose it will be necessary for you to make I desire that you would Remember the Ladies, and be more generous and favourable to them than your ancestors. Do not put such unlimited power into the hands of the Husbands. Remember all Men would be tyrants if they could. If perticular care and attention is not paid to the Ladies we are determined to foment a Rebelion, and will not hold ourselves bound by any Laws in which we have no voice, or Representation.

That your sex are Naturally Tyrannical is a Truth so thoroughly established as to admit of no dispute, but such of you as wish to be happy willingly give up the harsh title of Master for the more tender and endearing one of Friend. Why then, not put it out of the power of the vicious and the Lawless to use us with cruelty and indignity with impunity. Men of Sense in all Ages abhor those customs which treat us only as the vassals of your Sex. Regard us then as Beings placed by providence under your protection and in imitation of the Supreme Being make use of that power only for our happiness.

John Adams to Abigail Adams

April 14, 1776

As to your extraordinary Code of Laws, I cannot but laugh. We have been told that our Struggle has loosened the bands of Government every where. That Children and Apprentices were disobedient—that schools and Colledges were grown turbulent—that Indians slighted their Guardians and Negroes grew insolent to their Masters. But your Letter was the first Intimation that another Tribe more numerous and powerfull than all the rest were grown discontented. This is rather too coarse a Compliment but you are so saucy, I wont blot it out.

Depend upon it, We know better than to repeal our Masculine systems. Altho they are in Full Force, you know they are little more than Theory. We dare not exert our Power in its full Latitude. We are obliged to go fair, and softly, and in Practice you know We are the subjects. We have only the Name of Masters, and rather than give up this, which would compleatly subject Us to the Despotism of the Peticoat, I hope General Washington, and all our brave Heroes would fight. I am sure every good Politician would plot, as long as he would against Despotism, Empire, Monarchy, Aristocracy, Oligarchy, or Ochlocracy.

Name _____

Remember the Ladies Letters—
Reader's Theater

For the Girls

R1 and R2: Abigail Adams to John Adams, March 31, 1776

R1:   I long to hear that you have declared an independancy—

R2:   and by the way in the new Code of Laws which I suppose it will be necessary for you to make

R1 and R2: I desire that you would Remember the Ladies,

R1:   and be more generous and favourable to them than your ancestors.

R2:   Do not put such unlimited power into the hands of the Husbands.

R1 and R2: Remember all Men would be tyrants if they could.

R1:   If perticular care and attention is not paid to the Ladies we are determined to foment a Rebelion,

R2:   and will not hold ourselves bound by any Laws in which we have no voice, or Representation.

R1:   That your sex are Naturally Tyrannical is a Truth so thoroughly established as to admit of no dispute,

R2:   but such of you as wish to be happy willingly give up the harsh title of Master for the more tender and endearing one of Friend.

R1:   Why then, not put it out of the power of the vicious and the Lawless to use us with cruelty and indignity with impunity.

R2:   Men of Sense in all Ages abhor those customs which treat us only as the vassals of your Sex.

R1:   Regard us then as Beings

R2:   placed by providence

R1:   under your protection

R2:   and in imitation of the Supreme Being

R1 and R2: make use of that power only for our happiness.

Remember the Ladies Letters— Reader's Theater *(cont.)*

For the Boys

R1 and R2: John Adams to Abigail Adams, April 14, 1776

R1:   As to your extraordinary Code of Laws, I cannot but laugh.

R2:   We have been told that our Struggle has loosened the bands of Government

R1 and R2: every where.

R1:   That Children and Apprentices were disobedient—

R2:   that schools and Colledges were grown turbulent—

R1:   that Indians slighted their Guardians

R2:   and Negroes grew insolent to their Masters.

R1:   But your Letter was the first Intimation that another Tribe more numerous and powerfull than all the rest were grown discontented.

R2:   This is rather too coarse a Compliment but you are so saucy, I wont blot it out.

R1 and R2: Depend upon it,

R1:   We know better than to repeal our Masculine systems.

R2:   Altho they are in Full Force, you know they are little more than Theory.

R1 and R2: We dare not exert our Power in its full Latitude.

R1:   We are obliged to go fair,

R2:   and softly,

R1:   and in Practice you know We are the subjects.

R2:   We have only the Name of Masters, and rather than give up this,

R1:   which would compleatly subject Us to the Despotism of the Peticoat,

R2:   I hope General Washington, and all our brave Heroes would fight.

R1:   I am sure every good Politician would plot,

R2:   as long as he would

R1 and R2: against Despotism, Empire, Monarchy, Aristocracy, Oligarchy, or Ochlocracy.

Jefferson's Reaction to the Constitution

Objective

√ Students will participate in a cooperative learning activity to improve expressive reading skills by engaging in reader's theater.

Materials

- copy of *Reaction to the Constitution* (page 143) for the teacher
- copies of *Reaction to the Constitution—Reader's Theater* (pages 144–146) for the students

Fluency Suggestions and Activities

You may want to complete the history and/or vocabulary activities on the following page before this fluency activity. An understanding of the historical context and vocabulary will help students analyze and read the piece fluently.

1. Explain to the students that they will read the text for this lesson in the form of reader's theater. Review with the students that reader's theater is a shared reading activity, where several students take turns reading parts of text. Some parts of the selection are read by individual students, and some parts are read by all students.

2. Divide the students into groups of five and distribute copies of *Reaction to the Constitution—Reader's Theater* (pages 144–146). Assign each student in the group a part to read. Parts are labeled R1 (for Reader 1) to R5. Draw their attention to the parts to be read by "All" students. These are emphasized in bold print. Have the students discuss words or phrases that should carry particular expressive emphasis. Allow students time in class to practice their readings of the text.

3. Explain to the students that it will be necessary for the audience to have more background information about the Constitution in order to have a clear understanding of the reaction to it. To do this, they will research and create an introduction to their reader's theater. The introduction can be a short paragraph read by one of the group members or it can be presented in reader's theater format.

4. Have students present their versions of the reading to class. Then, arrange to have students perform their readings publicly. You may want to arrange performances in the school library, at a parent event, or during a school assembly. You could time these presentations to celebrate Jefferson's birthday in April. Or, you could complete them around Constitution Day on September 17.

5. Have students write letters to Jefferson's home, Monticello, Virginia, telling the caretakers there what they have been doing in class. They could even send a video or audio tape of their public performances.

Jefferson's Reaction to the Constitution (cont.)

History Connection

Begin the lesson by providing the students with information about the Constitution. The text for this lesson is one man's reaction to the Constitution. Ask the students to think about and discuss what they think the remainder of the text will be about. Then ask: Why might people have objections to the Constitution? Should people be allowed to suggest changes to such a document? Do the states have a say in policies of the federal government today?

Ratifying the Constitution was not as simple as one might think. There were two sides to the debate and each side was very vocal with its opinions. The Federalists wanted to ratify the document as it was. They felt it would provide a strong government for the new country. The Anti-Federalists felt that the document was missing a very important part—a bill of rights. Without a bill of rights, the personal rights of the citizens could be abused by the government. Anti-Federalists fought against ratification until a promise was made to add a bill of rights. Thomas Jefferson was not part of the Constitutional Convention. So, when he returned to America and first read the document, his reaction was very strong. He was an Anti-Federalist who fought to have a bill of rights added.

Vocabulary Connection

Discuss unfamiliar vocabulary encountered in the text. Some possible words are listed below. After identifying the difficult words, discuss them within the context of the text.

- **sate**—to have a meeting
- **dissolution**—when something is finished
- **contemplated**—to think about
- **provisions**—plans
- **habeas corpus**—a document to keep citizens from having to go to court unfairly
- **reeligibility**—to be qualified to participate again
- **approbations**—approvals
- **tenures**—terms for holding or owning something
- **concurrence**—agreement
- **liability**—being legally responsible for something
- **restrained**—held back
- **disapprobation**—disagreement

Extension Idea

- Assign sections of the text to groups of students and instruct them to rewrite the text using today's language. Invite groups to read their rewritten text to the class and discuss its meaning.

Reaction to the Constitution

This Convention met at Philadelphia on the 25th of May '87. It sate with closed doors, and kept all its proceedings secret, until it's dissolution on the 17th of September, when the results of their labors were published all together. I received a copy early in November, and read and contemplated its provisions with great satisfaction. As not a member of the Convention however, nor probably a single citizen of the Union, had approved it in all its parts, so I too found articles which I thought objectionable.

The absence of express declarations ensuring freedom of religion, freedom of the press, freedom of the person under the uninterrupted protection of the Habeas corpus, & trial by jury in civil as well as in criminal cases excited my jealousy; and the re-eligibility of the President for life, I quite disapproved. I expressed freely in letters to my friends, and most particularly to Mr. Madison & General Washington, my approbations and objections. How the good should be secured, and the ill brought to rights was the difficulty. To refer it back to a new Convention might endanger the loss of the whole. My first idea was that the 9 states first acting should accept it unconditionally, and thus secure what in it was good, and that the 4 last should accept on the previous condition that certain amendments should be agreed to, but a better course was devised of accepting the whole and trusting that the good sense & honest intention of our citizens would make the alterations which should be deemed necessary. Accordingly all accepted, 6 without objection, and 7 with recommendations of specified amendments.

Those respecting the press, religion, & juries, with several others, of great value, were accordingly made; but the Habeas corpus was left to the discretion of Congress, and the amendment against the reeligibility of the President was not proposed by that body. My fears of that feature were rounded on the importance of the office, on the fierce contentions it might excite among ourselves, if continuable for life, and the dangers of interference either with money or arms, by foreign nations, to whom the choice of an American President might become interesting. Examples of this abounded in history; in the case of the Roman emperors for instance, of the Popes while of any significance, of the German emperors, the Kings of Poland, & the Deys of Barbary. I had observed too in the feudal History, and in the recent instance particularly of the Stadtholder of Holland, how easily offices or tenures for life slide into inheritances. My wish therefore was that the President should be elected for 7 years & be ineligible afterwards. This term I thought sufficient to enable him, with the concurrence of the legislature, to carry thro' & establish any system of improvement he should propose for the general good. But the practice adopted I think is better allowing his continuance for 8 years with a liability to be dropped at half way of the term, making that a period of probation. That his continuance should be restrained to 7 years was the opinion of the Convention at an early stage of its session, when it voted that term by a majority of 8 against 2 and by a simple majority that he should be ineligible a second time. This opinion &c. was confirmed by the house so late as July 26, referred to the committee of detail, rereported favorably by them, and changed to the present form by final vote on the last day but one only of their session. Of this change three states expressed their disapprobation, N. York by recommending an amendment that the President should not be eligible a third time, and Virginia and N. Carolina that he should not be capable of serving more than 8 in any term of 16 years. And altho' this amendment has not been made in form, yet practice seems to have established it. The example of 4 Presidents voluntarily retiring at the end of their 8th year, & the progress of public opinion that the principle is salutary, have given it in practice the force of precedent & usage; insomuch that should a President consent to be a candidate for a 3rd election, I trust he would be rejected on this demonstration of ambitious views.

Name _____

Reaction to the Constitution—
Reader's Theater

R1:   This Convention met in Philadelphia on May 25, 1887.

R2:   It met with closed doors, and kept all its proceedings secret, until the meeting ended on September 17,

R3:   when the results of their labors were published.

R4:   I received a copy early in November, and read and contemplated it with great satisfaction.

R5:   No one at the Convention or any other citizen of the Union had approved it in all its parts, so I too found articles which I thought

All: objectionable.

R1:   The absence of specific declarations ensuring

R2:   freedom of religion,

R3:   freedom of the press,

R4:   freedom of each person for a fair trial

R5:   and trial by jury in civil as well as in criminal cases

All: excited my jealousy;

R1:   and the re-eligibility of the President for life,

All: I quite disapproved.

R2:   I expressed freely in letters to my friends,

R3:   and most particularly to Mr. Madison & General Washington, what I liked and disliked.

R4:   How the good parts of the document should be saved while the bad parts were changed was the difficulty.

Reaction to the Constitution— Reader's Theater *(cont.)*

R5: To refer it back to a new Convention might endanger the loss of the whole.

R1: My first idea was that nine states should accept it unconditionally,

R2: and secure what in it was good. Then, four should accept it with the condition that certain amendments should be passed immediately.

R3: But a better course was devised of accepting the whole and trusting that the

All: **good sense and honest intention of our citizens would make the necessary changes.**

R4: Accordingly all accepted, six without objection, and seven with recommendations of specified amendments.

R5: Amendments respecting the press, religion, and juries, with several others of great value, were made;

R1: but the Habeas corpus was left to the discretion of Congress, and the amendment against the reeligibility of the President was not proposed by that body.

R2: My fears of the reeligibility of the President were based on the importance of the office, on the fierce competition it might cause,

R3: if men could stay in office for life, and the dangers of interference, by foreign nations,

R4: to whom the choice of an American President might become interesting.

R5: There are many examples of this in history;

R1: the Roman emperors for instance,

R2: or the Popes of any significance,

R3: or the German emperors,

R4: or the Kings of Poland,

Reaction to the Constitution— Reader's Theater *(cont.)*

R5:   I had also observed in the feudal history,

R1:   how easily offices or jobs for life slide into inheritances.

R2:   My wish therefore was that the President should be elected for seven years and be ineligible afterwards.

R3:   This term I thought was long enough to enable him, with the agreement of the legislature,

R4:   to carry through and establish any system of improvement he wants for the general good.

R5:   But the practice adopted I think is better allowing his continuance for eight years with the ability to be dropped half way through the term,

R1:   making that a period of probation.

R2:   Of this change three states expressed their disagreement,

R3:   New York by recommending an amendment that the President should not be eligible a third time,

R4:   and Virginia and North Carolina that he should not be capable of serving more than eight in any term of sixteen years.

R5:   And although this amendment has not been made in form, practice seems to have established it.

R1:   The example of presidents voluntarily retiring at the end of their eighth year,

R2:   has given it in practice the force of precedent and usage;

R3:   if a president tries to be a candidate for a third election,

All: **I trust he would be rejected on this demonstration of ambitious views.**

Thomas Jefferson Writes

Objective

√ Students will deliver a group oral presentation and read passages fluently after practicing and monitoring fluency with repeated readings.

Materials

- copies of *Writing the Declaration of Independence* (pages 152–155) for the students
- copies *Fluency Progress Graph* (page 156), one for each student

Fluency Suggestions and Activities

You may want to complete the history and/or vocabulary activities on the following page before this fluency activity. An understanding of the historical context and vocabulary will help students analyze and read the piece fluently.

1. Explain that for this lesson, students will read text after practicing it and record the number of words read in a designated period of time. For your reference, the original texts (*Documents about Writing the Declaration of Independence*) are provided on pages 149–151. The copies that you will want to give to your students, *Writing the Declaration of Independence*, are on pages 152–155.

2. Each section of the writings has a reading level and number of words listed in the table below. Assign appropriate sections to students based on their reading levels.

Passage	Reading Level	Word Count
1	8.9	165
2	5.8	201
3	5.6	247
4	2.9	107
5	4.4	126
6	5.2	91
7	6.5	138
8	5.4	92
9	6.3	119

Reading Rate Goals	
Third grade	100
Fourth grade	110
Fifth grade	120
Sixth grade (and higher)	140

3. You may need to assign more than one section to a student in order to have enough text for him or her to read for the one-minute timed reading (described below). (Note that these passages have been rewritten to achieve various reading levels.) Provide time in class for the students to practice reading their passages.

4. Have a student read aloud for exactly one minute and make a mark where he or she stopped reading. Then have the student read the passage(s) again for one minute, and again note the stopping point. Count the total number of words the student read in the passage(s) during both readings. Divide by two to get the average number of words read per minute (WPM). Determine the number of words read incorrectly in both readings. Divide by two to get the average number of errors per minute. Subtract the average number of errors per minute from the average WPM to get the words correct per minute (WCPM). Record the date and the WCPM on the student's *Fluency Progress Graph* (page 156). Repeat this process a few times during the school year to assess each student's progress. See the chart above for average reading rate goals. (Reading Rate Goals from *The Fluent Reader: Oral Reading Strategies for Building Word Recognition, Fluency, and Comprehension*, by Timothy V. Rasinksi. Scholastic, 2003.)

Thomas Jefferson Writes *(cont.)*

History Connection

Introduce the text for the lesson by sharing the information about the Declaration of Independence provided below. Explain that these writings are documentation about the process of writing the Declaration of Independence.

Congress chose a committee of five men to write the Declaration. The committee met to discuss how to handle this important job. They decided it would be too hard to write as a group. Instead they decided to have one person write the essay. Then they would all meet to go over it together. Jefferson had written some important papers in the past. The committee knew he was a gifted writer. So, they chose him to write the document.

The committee made a smart choice when it picked Thomas Jefferson to write the document. He was a great writer. He was also very excited about the subject. Jefferson came to believe that freedom was something that people could not live without. He was happy when the other members of Congress finally agreed with him. For more than two weeks, Jefferson worked on his essay. During that time, he rarely spoke to anyone. He used all his energy to write. He wanted the words to be so powerful that everyone would agree with them.

Vocabulary Connection

Discuss unfamiliar vocabulary encountered in the text. Some possible words are listed below. After identifying the difficult words, discuss them within the context of the text.

- **prudent**—to have good judgment
- **alliance**—to have a connection with something
- **zeal**—enthusiastism
- **scrutiny**—to look at something very carefully
- **oratorical**—relating to an oral speech
- **vehement**—intensely emotional
- **philippic**—a speech or piece of writing that is full of blame
- **venture**—give an opinion knowing that people may disagree
- **interlined**—to add notes to a something that has already been written
- **sentiment**—a feeling

Extension Idea

- Invite students who would like a greater challenge to practice and possibly memorize portions of these notes and letters. Encourage them to recite the lines of the text with the conviction and confidence these men would have expressed.

Documents about Writing the Declaration of Independence

Jefferson's Autobiography

It appearing in the course of these debates that the colonies of N. York, New Jersey, Pennsylvania, Delaware, Maryland, and South Carolina were not yet matured for falling from the parent stem, but that they were fast advancing to that state, it was thought most prudent to wait a while for them, and to postpone the final decision to July 1, but that this might occasion as little delay as possible a committee was appointed to prepare a declaration of independence. The commee were J. Adams, Dr. Franklin, Roger Sherman, Robert R. Livingston & myself. Committees were also appointed at the same time to prepare a plan of confederation for the colonies, and to state the terms proper to be proposed for foreign alliance. The committee for drawing the declaration of Independence desired me to do it. It was accordingly done, and being approved by them, I reported it to the house on Friday the 28th of June when it was read and ordered to lie on the table.

Autobiography of John Adams

The committee had several meetings, in which were proposed the articles of which the declaration was to consist, and minutes made of them. The committee then appointed Mr. Jefferson and me to draw them up in form, and clothe them in a proper dress. The sub-committee met, and considered the minutes, making such observations on them as then occurred, when Mr. Jefferson desired me to take them to my lodgings, and make the draught. This I declined, and gave several reasons for declining, 1. That he was a Virginian, and I a Massachusettensian. 2. That he was a southern man, and I a northern one. 3. That I had been so obnoxious for my early and constant zeal in promoting the measure, that any draught of mine would undergo a more severe scrutiny and criticism in Congress, than one of his composition. 4. And lastly, and that would be reason enough if there were no other, I had a great opinion of the elegance of his pen, and none at all of my own. I therefore insisted that no hesitation should be made on his part. He accordingly took the minutes, and in a day or two produced to me his draught. Whether I made or suggested any correction, I remember not. The report was made to the committee of five, by them examined, but, whether altered or corrected in any thing, I cannot recollect. But, in substance at least, it was reported to Congress, where, after a severe criticism, and striking out several of the most oratorical paragraphs, it was adopted on the fourth of July, 1776, and published to the world.

Documents about Writing the Declaration of Independence *(cont.)*

Letter from John Adams to Timothy Pickering, August 22, 1822

You inquire why so young a man as Mr. Jefferson was placed at the head of the Committee for preparing a Declaration of Independence? I answer: it was the Frankfort advice, to place Virginia at the head of every thing. Mr. Richard Henry Lee might be gone to Virginia, to his sick family, for aught I know, but that was not the reason of Mr. Jefferson's appointment. There were three committees appointed at the same time. One for the Declaration of Independence, another for preparing the articles of Confederation, another for preparing a treaty to be proposed to France. Mr. Lee was chosen for the committee of Confederation, and it was not thought convenient that the same person should be upon both. Mr. Jefferson came into Congress, in June, 1775, and brought with him a reputation for literature, science, and a happy talent of composition. Writings of his were handed about, remarkable for the peculiar felicity of expression. Though a silent member in Congress, he was so prompt, frank, explicit, and decisive upon committees and in conversation, not even Samuel Adams was more so, that he soon seized upon my heart and upon this occasion I gave him my vote, and did all in my power to procure the votes of others. I think he had one more vote than any other, and that placed him at the head of the committee. I had the next highest number, and that placed me the second. The committee met, discussed the subject, and then appointed Mr. Jefferson and me to make the draft, I suppose because we were the two first on the list.

The sub-committee met. Jefferson proposed to me to make the draft. I said: "I will not." "You should do it." "Oh! no." "Why will you not? You ought to do it." "I will not." "Why?" "Reasons enough." "What can be your reasons?"

"Reason first—You are a Virginian, and a Virginian ought to appear at the head of this business. Reason second—I am obnoxious, suspected, and unpopular. You are very much otherwise. Reason third—You can write ten times better than I can."

"Well," said Jefferson, "If you are decided, I will do as well as I can."

"Very well. When you have drawn it up, we will have a meeting."

A meeting we accordingly had, and conned the paper over. I was delighted with its high tone and the flights of oratory with which it abounded, especially that concerning negro slavery, which, though I knew his Southern brethren would never suffer to pass in Congress, I certainly never would oppose. There were other expressions which I would not have inserted, if I had drawn it up, particularly that which called the King tyrant. I thought this too personal; for I never believed George to be a tyrant in disposition and in nature; I always believed him to be deceived by his courtiers on both sides of the Atlantic, and in his official capacity only, cruel. I thought the expression too passionate, and too much like scolding, for so grave and solemn a document; but as Franklin and Sherman were to inspect it afterwards, I thought it would not become me to strike it out. I consented to report it, and do not now remember that I made or suggested a single alteration.

We reported it to the committee of five. It was read, and I do not remember that Franklin or Sherman criticised any thing. We were all in haste. Congress was impatient, and the instrument was reported, as I believe, in Jefferson's handwriting, as he first drew it. Congress cut off about a quarter of it, as I expected they would; but they obliterated some of the best of it, and left all that was exceptionable, if anything in it was. I have long wondered that the original draught has not been published. I suppose the reason is, the vehement philippic against negro slavery.

Documents about Writing the Declaration of Independence *(cont.)*

Letter from Jefferson to James Madison, August 30, 1823

You have doubtless seen Timothy Pickering's fourth of July observations on the Declaration of Independence. If his principles and prejudices, personal and political, gave us no reason to doubt whether he had truly quoted the information he alleges to have received from Mr. Adams, I should then say, that in some of the particulars, Mr. Adams' memory has led him into unquestionable error. At the age of eighty-eight, and forty-seven years after the transactions of Independence, this is not wonderful. Nor should I, at the age of eighty, on the small advantage of that difference only, venture to oppose my memory to his, were it not supported by written notes, taken by myself at the moment and on the spot.

Says 'the committee of five, to wit, Doctor Franklin, Sherman, Livingston and ourselves, met, discussed the subject, and then appointed him and myself to make the draught; that we, as a sub-committee, met, and after the urgencies of each on the other, I consented to undertake the task, that the draught being made, we, the sub-committee, met, and conned the paper over, and he does not remember that he made or suggested a single alteration.' Now these details are quite incorrect.

The committee of five met; no such thing as a sub-committee was proposed, but they unanimously pressed on myself alone to undertake the draught. I consented; I drew it; but before I reported it to the committee, I communicated it separately to Doctor Franklin and Mr. Adams, requesting their corrections because they were the two members of whose judgments and amendments I wished most to have the benefit, before presenting it to the committee: and you have seen the original paper now in my hands, with the corrections of Doctor Franklin and Mr. Adams interlined in their own handwritings. Their alterations were two or three only, and merely verbal. I then wrote a fair copy, reported it to the committee, and from them unaltered, to Congress. This personal communication and consultation with Mr. Adams, he has misremembered into the actings of a sub-committee.

Pickering's observations, and Mr. Adams' in addition, "that it contained no new ideas, that it is a common place compilation, its sentiments hacknied in Congress for two years before, and its essence contained in Otis' pamphlet," may all be true. Of that I am not to be the judge. Richard Henry Lee charged it as copied from Locke's treatise on government. Otis' pamphlet I never saw, and whether I had gathered my ideas from reading or reflection I do not know. I know only that I turned to neither book nor pamphlet while writing it. I did not consider it as any part of my charge to invent new ideas altogether, and to offer no sentiment which had ever been expressed before.

Writing the Declaration of Independence

Passage 1

Jefferson's Autobiography

It appears that in the course of these debates that the colonies of New York, New Jersey, Pennsylvania, Delaware, Maryland, and South Carolina were not yet matured for falling from the parent stem. They were fast advancing to that state. It was thought most prudent to wait a while for them, and to postpone the final decision to July 1. But that this might occasion as little delay as possible a committee was appointed to prepare a declaration of independence. The committee were John Adams, Dr. Franklin, Roger Sherman, Robert Livingston, and myself. Committees were also appointed at the same time to make a plan of confederation for the colonies, and to state the terms proper to be proposed for foreign alliance. The committee for drawing the declaration of Independence desired me to do it. It was done. After being approved by them, I reported it to the house on Friday the 28th of June. It was read and ordered to lie on the table.

Passage 2

Autobiography of John Adams

The committee had several meetings. Articles were proposed of which the declaration was to consist, and minutes made of them. The committee then appointed Mr. Jefferson and me to draw them up in form, and clothe them in a proper dress. The sub-committee met and considered the minutes. They made observations about them. When Mr. Jefferson desired me to take them to my lodgings, and make the draft. This I declined for several reasons. First, he was from Virginia. I am from Massachusetts. Second, he was a southern man. I am a northern man. Third, I had been obnoxious for my early excitement in promoting the measure. Any draft of mine would undergo a more severe scrutiny. It would be criticized more in Congress. Fourth, I like his writing better than my own. I therefore insisted that no hesitation should be made on his part. He took the minutes, and in a day or two gave me his draft. I don't remember making any corrections. The report was given to the committee. I cannot remember if they made any changes to it. It was then reported to Congress. After great criticism, it was adopted on the fourth of July 1776, and published to the world.

Writing the Declaration of Independence *(cont.)*

Passage 3

Letter from John Adams to Timothy Pickering, August 22, 1822

You ask why so young a man as Mr. Jefferson was placed at the head of the Committee for preparing a Declaration of Independence? It was the Frankfort advice, to place Virginia at the head of every thing. Mr. Richard Henry Lee might be gone to Virginia, to his sick family. But that was not the reason of Mr. Jefferson's appointment. There were three committees appointed at the same time. One for the Declaration of Independence. Another was for preparing the articles of Confederation. Another was for preparing a treaty to be proposed to France. Mr. Lee was chosen for the committee of Confederation.

It wasn't convenient that the same person should be upon both. Mr. Jefferson came into Congress, in June, 1775. He brought with him a reputation for literature, science, and a talent of writing. Writings of his were handed about. They were remarkable. Though a silent member in Congress, he was honest, direct, and always on time, And he made good decisions. He soon won my respect. I gave him my vote. And I did all in my power to get him the votes of others. I think he had one more vote than any other. That placed him at the head of the committee. I had the next highest number. That placed me the second. The committee met and discussed the subject. They appointed Mr. Jefferson and me to make the draft. I suppose because we were the two first on the list.

Passage 4

Letter from John Adams to Timothy Pickering *(cont.)*

The sub-committee met. Jefferson asked to me to make the draft. I said: "I will not."

"You should do it."

"Oh! no."

"Why will you not? You ought to do it."

"I will not."

"Why?"

"Reasons enough."

"What can be your reasons?"

"Reason first—You are a Virginian. A Virginian ought to appear at the head of this business. Reason second—I am obnoxious and unpopular. You are very much otherwise. Reason third—You can write ten times better than I can."

"Well," said Jefferson, "If you are decided, I will do as well as I can."

"Very well. When you have drawn it up, we will have a meeting."

Writing the Declaration of Independence (cont.)

Passage 5

Letter from John Adams to Timothy Pickering (cont.)

We had a meeting to discuss the paper. I was happy with it. I really liked the part about negro slavery. I knew his Southern brothers would never pass it in Congress. I would never disagree. There were other expressions which I would not have used. I would not have called the King tyrant. I thought this too personal. I never believed George to be a tyrant. I always believed him to be fooled by others. I thought the expression too passionate. It was too much like scolding. But as Franklin and Sherman were to inspect it afterwards, I thought it would not become me to strike it out. I approved the report, and do not now remember that I made or suggested a single alteration.

Passage 6

Letter from John Adams to Timothy Pickering (cont.)

We reported it to the committee of five. It was read. I do not remember that Franklin or Sherman criticised anything. We were all in a hurry. Congress was impatient. The instrument was reported, as I believe, in Jefferson's handwriting. Congress cut off about a quarter of it, as I thought they would. But they destroyed some of the best of it. They left all that was exceptionable. I have long wondered that the original draft has not been published. I think the reason is, the strong position against negro slavery.

Writing the Declaration of Independence (cont.)

Passage 7

Letter from Jefferson to James Madison, August 30, 1823

You have seen Timothy Pickering's fourth of July observations on the Declaration of Independence. I say, he is mistaken. I am eighty-eight years old. Forty-seven years after the transactions of Independence, this is not wonderful. At my age, I should not oppose my memory to his. But I have notes, taken by myself at the moment and on the spot. He says 'the committee of five, to wit, Doctor Franklin, Sherman, Livingston and ourselves, met, discussed the subject. Then we appointed him and myself to make the draft. He said that we, as a sub-committee, met, and after the urgencies of each on the other, I agreed to write the draft. He said the sub-committee, met, and reviewed the paper. He said he does not remember that he suggested a single change. These details are not correct.

Passage 8

Letter from Jefferson to James Madison (cont.)

The committee of five met. No such thing as a sub-committee was proposed. They all asked me to write the draft. I agreed. I wrote it. But before I reported it to the committee, I communicated it to Doctor Franklin and Mr. Adams. I asked for their corrections because I respected their judgments. I wanted their comments before presenting it to the committee. They suggested only two and three changes. I then wrote another copy. This I reported to the committee and then to Congress. Mr. Adams did not remember this correctly.

Passage 9

Letter from Jefferson to James Madison (cont.)

Pickering said, "that it contained no new ideas, that it is a common place compilation, its sentiments hacknied in Congress for two years before, and its essence contained in Otis' pamphlet." This may all be true. I am not to judge that. Richard Henry Lee said it was copied from Locke's treatise on government. Otis' pamphlet I never saw. Whether I had gathered my ideas from reading or reflection I do not know. I know only that I did not turn to a book nor a pamphlet while writing it. I did not consider it as any part of my charge to invent new ideas altogether. I was not to offer no sentiment which had ever been expressed before.

Name _____

Fluency Progress Graph

Directions: Use the graph below to track a student's fluency progress. Calculate words correct per minute (WCPM) and plot fluency readings throughout the year. This will provide a visual record of progress to show to parents.

Words Correct Per Minute (WCPM)

150							
140							
130							
120							
110							
100							
90							
80							
70							
60							
50							
40							
30							
20							
Date							

George and Martha Washington

Objective

√ Students will deliver a group oral presentation and read passages fluently after practicing and monitoring fluency with repeated readings.

Materials

- copies of *Letter to Martha Washington* (page 159) for the students
- two PVC elbow joints per student; short lengths of straight PVC pipe for each student
- copy of *Practice Makes Perfect* (page 160) for the teacher

Fluency Suggestions and Activities

You may want to complete the history and/or vocabulary activities on the following page before this fluency activity. An understanding of the historical context and vocabulary will help students analyze and read the piece fluently.

1. Begin the lesson by explaining that repeated reading of a text helps to increase fluency. Tell the students that they will have a unique way of practicing fluency in today's activity. Read the text of the *Letter to Martha Washington* (page 159) aloud, modeling fluent reading.

2. When all students practice fluency by reading aloud, the classroom can become quite noisy. To alleviate this problem, make individual telephone-like voice amplifiers using PVC pipe. To make a telephone, attach a PVC elbow joint to either end of a straight section of PVC pipe. Turn the elbows in the same direction, so one opening can be held by the ear, while the other opening is near the mouth. When the child speaks softly into the mouthpiece, his or her voice will be amplified in the earpiece.

3. Provide each student with a copy of the *Letter to Martha Washington* (page 159) and a PVC voice amplifier. Demonstrate how to hold the apparatus like a telephone receiver and speak softly into it. Allow the students to give it a try. Explain that they will use this apparatus to practice reading the text aloud multiple times in order to improve their fluency.

4. Allow students time in class to practice reading the text. As students practice, work with individual students to check their fluency progress.

5. Use *Practice Makes Perfect* (page 160) as a guide for selecting appropriate texts for the students and for identifying reading levels.

6. Have students present their readings to the class. Then arrange to have students perform their readings for the classes at their grade level. Time the presentations to coincide with Election Day or Washington's birthday in February.

George and Martha Washington (cont.)

History Connection

Introduce the letter to Martha Washington and discuss the historical information provided below.

In 1759, Washington married Martha Custis. They lived at Mount Vernon in Virginia. He wanted to farm and live peacefully with his wife and two stepchildren. Unfortunately for George and Martha, George's career kept him away from home for long periods of time. During their time apart, the couple wrote letters to each other. Before her death, Martha destroyed most of their letters. So, unlike Abigail and John Adams, historians have not been able to learn a lot about the lives of this famous couple through their own words.

Vocabulary Connection

Discuss unfamiliar vocabulary encountered in the text. Some possible words are listed below. After identifying the difficult words, discuss them within the context of the text.

- **solemn**—serious
- **appointment**—position or job
- **endeavor**—effort
- **consciousness**—to know or be aware of something
- **capacity**—ability
- **prospect**—chance or possibility
- **abroad**—away from home
- **utterly**—totally
- **censure**—judgment or blame
- **providence**—guidance or care from God
- **heretofore**—up to this time
- **bountiful**—plentiful

Extension Idea

- Invite students who would like a greater challenge to practice more difficult texts using voice amplifiers.

Letter to Martha Washington

By George Washington

Martha,

It has been determined in Congress, that the whole army raised for the defence of the American cause shall be put under my care, and that it is necessary for me to proceed immediately to Boston to take upon me the command of it.

You may believe me, my dear Patsy, when I assure you in the most solemn manner that, so far from seeking this appointment, I have used every endeavor in my power to avoid it, not only from my unwillingness to part with you and the family, but from a consciousness of its being a trust too great for my capacity, and that I should enjoy more real happiness in one month with you at home than I have the most distant prospect of finding abroad . . . .

It was utterly out of my power to refuse this appointment, without exposing my character to such censure as would have reflected dishonor upon myself, and have given pain to my friends . . . .

I shall rely, therefore, confidently on that Providence which has heretofore preserved and been bountiful to me, not doubting but that I shall return safe to you in the fall.

George

Name _____

Practice Makes Perfect

Directions: Use these tips as guidelines for assessing your students' fluency progress.

Reading Levels

When working on fluency development, it is important to select text that is at students' independent reading levels. You will need to designate different passages for the students to ensure that they are working with text that is at the appropriate levels. The National Reading Panel (2000) suggests the following for determining reading levels:

- **Independent Level:** This refers to easy text in which only 1 in 20 words are difficult for the student. The student should have a 95% success rate.

- **Instructional Level:** This text is more challenging, but not too difficult. The student should only encounter 1 in 10 difficult words with a 90% success rate.

- **Frustration Level:** This level refers to text that is very challenging for the child, with more than 1 in 10 difficult words. The student would have less than a 90% rate of success.

Guide to Fluency Practice

- Be sure the student has selected a passage at his or her independent reading level. There should be no more than 1 in 20 difficult words.

- Ask the student to read the passage to you. (Pay attention to the student's reading rate, accuracy, and expression.)

- Assist the student in reading smoothly by modeling the reading of a sentence and then asking the child to repeat it.

- Try reading the passage together. Read at a comfortable rate and be sure to add expression.

- For more fluent readers, focus on the use of expression and a pleasing voice tone.

The National Reading Panel (2000). "Teaching Children to Read: An Evidence-Based Assessment of the Scientific Research Literature on Reading and Its Implications for Reading Instruction-Reports of Subgroups."

Washington's Farewell Speech

Objective

√ Students will participate in a cooperative learning activity to improve expressive reading skills by engaging in reader's theater.

Materials

- copy of *Excerpt from Washington's Farewell to His Armies* (page 163) for the teacher
- copies of *Washington's Farewell to His Armies—Reader's Theater* (pages 164–165) for the students
- video recorder and videotape

Fluency Suggestions and Activities

You may want to complete the history and/or vocabulary activities on the following page before this fluency activity. An understanding of the historical context and vocabulary will help students analyze and read the piece fluently.

1. Begin the lesson by explaining to students that they will be participating in a reader's theater activity. The text of this performance is a message from George Washington to the men in his armies.

2. Ask the students how Washington might have felt while saying goodbye to the faithful men in his military. How might his voice have reflected his feelings? Read the first two paragraphs of the *Excerpt from Washington's Farewell to His Armies* (page 163). Be sure to emphasize the mood Washington might have conveyed while reciting this speech.

3. Demonstrate to the students how expression and voice tone can dramatically change the performance by reading it once in monotone and once in a very exuberant, excited manner. Draw students' attention to the inappropriateness of no expression at all and too much expression.

4. Tell the students that they will perform the piece as a reader's theater in groups of five. Distribute copies of *Washington's Farewell to His Armies—Reader's Theater* (pages 164–165) to each group. Assign each student in the group a part to read. Remind them that parts are labeled R1 (for Reader 1) to R5. Draw their attention to the parts to be read by "All" students.

5. Have the students discuss words or phrases that should carry particular expressive emphasis and allow them time in class to practice their readings of the text.

6. Have students present their versions of the reading to the class. Make a videotape of the students' presentations and send them to Mount Vernon. Have students write letters to go with the videotape, explaining their project.

Washington's Farewell Speech *(cont.)*

History Connection

Discuss the historical information provided below to set the stage for this activity.

George Washington first served in a military role during the French and Indian War. He lead his troops so well during those engagements, that he was named the commander in chief of the Continental Army for the American Revolution. He was a well-loved and respected leader. At Valley Forge, instead of living separately from the men in comfortable housing, he showed them the kind of man he was by sleeping in the same cold, dirty cabins. On November 2, 1783, in an eloquent speech, he bid farewell to the men he led.

Vocabulary Connection

Discuss unfamiliar vocabulary encountered in the text. Some possible words are listed below. After identifying the difficult words, discuss them within the context of the text.

- **sovereignty**—when a country is not ruled by a king or queen who lives in a different country
- **inestimable**—when something is worth so much that it cannot be measured
- **acquisitions**—objects that have been gained
- **prudence**—when someone is well behaved and makes good decisions
- **inviolable**—not able to be doubted
- **adieu**—good bye
- **auspices**—guidance
- **benediction**—short blessing

Extension Idea

- When students have practiced the readings for their reader's theaters, have them perform for another group in your class. Encourage groups to offer one another constructive criticism to assist with the improvement of their performances.

Excerpt from Washington's Farewell to His Armies

By George Washington

It only remains for the Comdr in Chief to address himself once more, and that for the time, to the Armies of the U States . . . and to bid them an affectionate, a long farewell . . . .

It is universally acknowledged, that the enlarged prospects of happiness, opened by the conformation of our independence and sovereignty, almost exceeds the power of description. And shall not the brave men, who have contributed so essentially to these inestimable acquisitions, retiring victorious from the field of War to the field of agriculture, participate in all the blessings which have been obtained; in such a republic, who will exclude them from the rights of Citizens and the fruits of their labour?

The Commander in Chief conceives little is now wanting to enable the Soldiers to change the military character into that of the Citizen, but that steady and decent tenor of behavior which has generally distinguished, not only the Army under his immediate command, but the different detachments and separate Armies through the course of the war. From their good sense and prudence he anticipates the happiest consequences; and while he congratulates them on the glorious occasion, which renders their services in the field no longer necessary, he wishes to express the strong obligations he feels himself under for the assistance he has received from every Class, and in every instance . . . .

To the various branches of the Army the General takes this last and solemn opportunity of professing his inviolable attachment and friendship. He wishes more than bare professions were in his power, that he were really able to be useful to them all in future life . . . .

And being now to conclude these his last public Orders, to take his ultimate leave in a short time of the military character, and to bid a final adieu to the Armies he has so long had the honor to Command, he can only again offer in their behalf his recommendations to their grateful country, and his prayers to the God of Armies.

May ample justice be done them here, and may the choicest of heaven's favours, both here and hereafter, attend those who, under the divine auspices, have secured innumerable blessings for others; with these wishes, and this benediction, the Commander in Chief is about to retire from Service. The curtain of separation will soon be drawn, and the military scene to him will be closed forever.

Name _____

Washington's Farewell to His Armies— Reader's Theater

R1: It only remains for the commander in chief to address himself once more,

R2: to the Armies of the United States . . . to bid them an affectionate,

All: and a long farewell.

R3: Everybody realizes that the prospects of happiness

R4: we have because of our new independence,

R5: almost exceeds the power of description.

R1: And shall not the brave men, who have contributed so essentially to this happiness and independence,

R2: retiring victorious from the field of War to the field of agriculture,

R3: participate in all the blessings which have been obtained;

R4: in such a republic, who will exclude them from the rights of citizens and the fruits of their labor?

R5: The commander in chief believes the soldiers will be able to change from their military characters into that of citizens,

R1: using that steady and decent behavior that has generally distinguished, not only the army under his immediate command, but the different detachments and separate armies through the course of the war.

R2: From their good sense and wise decisions he anticipates the happiest consequences;

R3: and while he congratulates them on winning the war, which renders their services in the field no longer necessary,

R4: he wishes to express the strong obligations he feels himself under

Washington's Farewell to His Armies— Reader's Theater *(cont.)*

R5: for the assistance he has received from every soldier, and in every instance.

R1: To the various branches of the army the general takes this last and solemn opportunity of professing his strong attachment

All: and friendship.

R2: He wishes more than bare professions were in his power, that he were really able to be useful to them all in future life . . . .

R3: And being now to conclude these his last public orders,

R4: to take his ultimate leave in a short time of the military character,

R5: and to bid a final good bye to the armies he has so long had the honor to command,

R1: he can only again offer in their behalf his recommendations to their grateful country,

All: and his prayers to the God of Armies.

R2: May enough justice be done for them here,

R3: and may the choicest of heaven's favors, both here and hereafter,

R4: attend those who, under the divine guidance,

R5: have secured numerous blessings for others;

R1: with these wishes, and this short blessing, the commander in chief is about to retire from service.

All: The curtain of separation will soon be drawn, and the military scene to him will be closed forever.

The Bald Eagle

Objective

√ Students will determine the meaning of text and then participate in a public oral reading, focusing the use of appropriate expression.

Materials

• copies of *The Bald Eagle as an Emblem of America* (page 168) for the students
• copies of *Analyzing The Bald Eagle as an Emblem of America* (page 169) for the students
• copies of *An Emblem of America* (page 170) for the students

Fluency Suggestions and Activities

You may want to complete the history and/or vocabulary activities on the following page before this fluency activity. An understanding of the historical context and vocabulary will help students analyze and read the piece fluently.

1. Distribute copies of *The Bald Eagle as an Emblem of America* (page 168). Read the piece aloud, modeling fluent reading.

2. Ask the students if they agree or disagree with the author of the text. Divide students into groups to complete *Analyzing The Bald Eagle as an Emblem of America* (page 169).

3. Explain to students that as they read, they will focus on the use of expression. To prepare for this, ask the students the following questions: How does the author feel about the bald eagle as an emblem of our country? How would this feeling be expressed as the author might read the text? Which particular lines of the text should be emphasized to show the author's feelings?

4. Then write the following portion of the text on the board, using underlining where indicated.

   . . . you may have seen him perch'd on some dead Tree, near the River where, <u>too lazy to fish for himself</u>, he watches the Labour of the Fishing-Hawk; and, when that diligent Bird has at length taken a Fish, and is bearing it to his Nest for the support of his Mate and young ones, the Bald Eagle pursues him, <u>and takes it from him</u>.

5. Explain to the students that the underlined words indicate where emphasis should be placed by using expression. For example, "too lazy to fish for himself" could be read with a tone of disgust or disappointment. The words "and takes it from him" might be expressed with a tone of disbelief. Ask students to try reading this portion of the text, emphasizing the underlined phrases.

6. Allow students time in class to practice their readings of the text. Encourage them to underline other phrases that could be emphasized with expression to reflect the author's feelings.

7. Have students present their versions of the reading to class. Then have the class vote on whose rendition used the most appropriate and inspiring expression. Arrange to have this student read the text to the school over the loud speaker. Arrange this presentation to coincide with Thanksgiving week or to celebrate Franklin's birthday in January.

The Bald Eagle (cont.)

History Connection

Begin the lesson by asking students if they know which bird was chosen to be the emblem of America. Ask the students to tell what they know about the bald eagle and write their responses on the board. Have the students tell whether or not they think the bald eagle is a good representation of America. Then explain that some people throughout history have felt that another emblem would have been more appropriate. Introduce Franklin's writing about the bald eagle as an emblem of America and discuss its historical importance using the information below.

At the end of the war, Franklin worked to negotiate peace with Great Britain. The treaty was written in France. This treaty stated that the colonies were free from Great Britain. Franklin returned to America in 1785. He was upset to hear that the eagle had been chosen as America's symbol. He said that the eagle was dishonest and stole food from the hawk. He thought the turkey would have been a better choice!

Vocabulary Connection

Discuss unfamiliar vocabulary encountered in the text. Some possible words are listed below. After identifying the difficult words, discuss them within the context of the text.

- **moral**—relating to right or wrong
- **character**—describes how a person is seen to others
- **labour**—labor, work
- **diligent**—busy
- **bearing**—bringing
- **pursues**—follows or chases
- **injustice**—when something unfair has happened
- **sharping**—being corrupt
- **rank**—outright
- **withal**—with all, as well

Extension Idea

- Divide students into small groups to discuss other birds that might be better emblems of America than the bald eagle. Distribute copies of the activity sheet, *An Emblem of America* (page 170) to assist them. Instruct each group to write a rationale for the selection of its bird. Encourage students to practice reciting their rationale passages and then perform them at a presentation entitled, "Emblems for Our Country."

The Bald Eagle as an Emblem of America

**By Benjamin Franklin to his daughter, Sarah Bache
on January 26, 1784**

For my own part, I wish the Bald Eagle had not been chosen as the Representative of our Country; he is a Bird of bad moral Character; he does not get his living honestly; you may have seen him perch'd on some dead Tree, near the River where, too lazy to fish for himself, he watches the Labour of the Fishing-Hawk; and, when that diligent Bird has at length taken a Fish, and is bearing it to his Nest for the support of his Mate and young ones, the Bald Eagle pursues him, and takes it from him. With all this Injustice he is never in good Case; but, like those among Men who live by Sharping and Robbing, he is generally poor, and often very lousy. Besides, he is a rank Coward; the little KingBird, not bigger than a Sparrow, attacks him boldly and drives him out of the District. He is therefore by no means a proper emblem for the brave and honest Country of America, who have driven all the kingbirds from our country.

For in truth, the turkey is in comparison a much more respectable bird, and withal a true original native of America. Eagles have been found in all countries, but the turkey was peculiar to ours; the first of the species seen in Europe, being brought to France by the Jesuits from Canada, and served up at the wedding table of Charles the Ninth. He is, besides (though a little vain and silly, it is true, but not the worse emblem for that) a bird of courage, and would not hesitate to attack a grenadier of the British guards, who should presume to invade his farmyard with a red coat on.

Name _____

Analyzing the Bald Eagle as an Emblem of America

Directions: Meet with your classmates to answer the questions below.

1. What does the bald eagle do that isn't honest?

   _____

   _____

   _____

2. What does this communicate about the "character" of the bald eagle?

   _____

   _____

   _____

3. The author suggests the turkey as a better emblem of America. What two reasons does the author give for this choice?

   _____

   _____

   _____

   _____

4. List other qualities of the turkey. Why do you agree or disagree with the turkey as an American emblem?

   _____

   _____

   _____

   _____

   _____

   _____

   _____

   _____

   _____

Name _____

An Emblem of America

Directions: What bird do you think would be a better emblem of American than the bald eagle? As a group, choose a bird and then complete this page.

1. What bird did your group select?

   _____

2. List the qualities of the bird your group selected.

   _____

   _____

3. How do these qualities represent our country?

   _____

   _____

   _____

   _____

   _____

4. Research the bird you selected using the Internet or resource books from the library. List some important information you find about the bird.

   _____

   _____

   _____

   _____

   _____

5. On another sheet of paper, write a one-paragraph statement about why your group's bird would make a good emblem of America.

Benjamin Franklin

Objective

√ Students will practice reading aloud portions of text in preparation for public performances.

Materials

- copy of the short story "Young Benjamin Franklin" (pages 173–174) for the teacher
- copies of *"Young Benjamin Franklin"—Divided Reading* (pages 175–179) for the students
- copies of *The Life of Benjamin Franklin* (page 180) for the students

Fluency Suggestions and Activities

You may want to complete the history and/or vocabulary activities on the following page before this fluency activity. An understanding of the historical context and vocabulary will help students analyze and read the piece fluently.

Note: Before the lesson begins, arrange to have students read a section of the story each day of the week over the loud speaker for the school.

1. Introduce the short story, "Young Benjamin Franklin" (pages 173–174), and read it aloud to model fluency. Explain that the students will have the opportunity to read the story in five sections over the school's loudspeaker.

2. Distribute copies of *"Young Benjamin Franklin"—Divided Reading* (pages 175–179) to students. Tell the students that in the days before television, people listened to the reading of stories on the radio. It was the responsibility of the radio storytellers to communicate the message and emotion of the story merely by using their voices.

3. Divide students into groups of four or five. Assign a section of the story to each group. Have the students in each group read through their section of the story. Then have them divide the text into parts for each student in the group. (See example below for Monday.)

   R1: When Benjamin Franklin was a boy he was very fond of fishing; and many of his leisure hours were spent on the margin of the mill pond catching flounders, perch, and eels that came up thither with the tide.

   R2: The place where Ben and his playmates did most of their fishing was a marshy spot on the outskirts of Boston.

   R3: On the edge of the water there was a deep bed of clay, in which the boys were forced to stand while they caught their fish.

   R4: "This is very uncomfortable," said Ben Franklin one day to his comrades, while they were standing in the quagmire.

   R5: "So it is," said the other boys. "What a pity we have no better place to stand!"

4. Remind the students to think about how to use their voices to make the story interesting, with particular expression added to dialogue in the story. Allow the students several days in class to practice the reading of their sections of the story. To practice their presentations, have students present their sections of the story to the rest of the class. Encourage classmates to offer suggestions for improved fluency.

Benjamin Franklin (cont.)

Fluency Suggestions and Activities (cont.)

5. Shortly before the performance week, have each group add a few sentences before and after the text to introduce and to conclude the reading. For example, the students on Monday might introduce the story by saying, "Each day this week, the students from Miss Johnson's class will be reading part of a story called 'Young Benjamin Franklin.' It is based on a short story written by Nathaniel Hawthorne." Then after the reading, a student may read a sentence, such as, "That concludes today's portion of the story. Tune in tomorrow for more of the story." On Tuesday, the students recap the previous day's reading, such as "Yesterday we began the reading of 'Young Benjamin Franklin.' You may remember that Benjamin and his friends were fishing. They were looking for a place to stand in order to stay dry. Here's the next part of the story."

History Connection

Begin the lesson by explaining to the students that this lesson focuses on a piece of writing based on a story by Nathaniel Hawthorne, a famous writer. Tell them that this piece is in the form of a story about Benjamin Franklin when he was a boy. Ask the students to tell what they know about Benjamin Franklin already.

Vocabulary Connection

Discuss unfamiliar vocabulary encountered in the text. Some possible words are listed below. After identifying the difficult words, discuss them within the context of the text.

- **thither**—to that place
- **comrades**—friends
- **quagmire**—a bog or marsh
- **bedaubed**—smeared
- **plight**—difficult situation
- **enterprise**—project
- **masons**—skilled workers
- **magistrate**—a person who works in a court of law
- **reproof**—criticism
- **hither**—here

Extension Idea

- Divide students into small groups to discuss the life of Benjamin Franklin. Distribute copies of the activity sheet, *The Life of Benjamin Franklin* (page 180), and allow the students time to discuss, research, and answer the questions.

Young Benjamin Franklin

This is based on a story written by Nathaniel Hawthorne.

When Benjamin Franklin was a boy he was very fond of fishing; and many of his leisure hours were spent on the margin of the mill pond catching flounders, perch, and eels that came up thither with the tide.

The place where Ben and his playmates did most of their fishing was a marshy spot on the outskirts of Boston. On the edge of the water there was a deep bed of clay, in which the boys were forced to stand while they caught their fish.

"This is very uncomfortable," said Ben Franklin one day to his comrades, while they were standing in the quagmire.

"So it is," said the other boys. "What a pity we have no better place to stand!"

On the dry land, not far from the quagmire, there were at that time a great many large stones that had been brought there to be used in building the foundation of a new house. Ben mounted upon the highest of these stones.

"Boys," said he, "I have thought of a plan. You know what a plague it is to have to stand in the quagmire yonder. See, I am bedaubed to the knees, and you are all in the same plight.

"Now I propose that we build a wharf. You see these stones? The workmen mean to use them for building a house here. My plan is to take these same stones, carry them to the edge of the water, and build a wharf with them. What say you, lads? Shall we build the wharf?"

"Yes, yes," cried the boys; "let's set about it!"

It was agreed that they should all be on the spot that evening, and begin their grand public enterprise by moonlight.

Accordingly, at the appointed time, the boys met and eagerly began to remove the stones. They worked like a colony of ants, sometimes two or three of them taking hold of one stone; and at last they had carried them all away, and built their little wharf.

"Now, boys," cried Ben, when the job was done, "let's give three cheers, and go home to bed. To-morrow we may catch fish at our ease."

"Hurrah! hurrah! hurrah!" shouted his comrades, and all scampered off home and to bed, to dream of to-morrow's sport.

In the morning the masons came to begin their work. But what was their surprise to find the stones all gone! The master mason, looking carefully on the ground, saw the tracks of many little feet, some with shoes and some barefoot. Following these to the water side, he soon found what had become of the missing building stones.

Young Benjamin Franklin *(cont.)*

"Ah! I see what the mischief is," said he; "those little rascals who were here yesterday have stolen the stones to build a wharf. And I must say that they understand their business well."

He was so angry that he at once went to make a complaint before the magistrate; and his Honor wrote an order to "take the bodies of Benjamin Franklin, and other evil-disposed persons," who had stolen a heap of stones.

If the owner of the stolen property had not been more merciful than the master mason, it might have gone hard with our friend Benjamin and his comrades. But, luckily for them, the gentleman had a respect for Ben's father, and, moreover, was pleased with the spirit of the whole affair. He therefore let the culprits off easily.

But the poor boys had to go through another trial, and receive sentence, and suffer punishment, too, from their own fathers. Many a rod was worn to the stump on that unlucky night. As for Ben, he was less afraid of a whipping than of his father's reproof. And, indeed, his father was very much disturbed.

"Benjamin, come hither," began Mr. Franklin in his usual stern and weighty tone. The boy approached and stood before his father's chair. "Benjamin," said his father, "what could induce you to take property which did not belong to you?"

"Why, father," replied Ben, hanging his head at first, but then lifting his eyes to Mr. Franklin's face, "if it had been merely for my own benefit, I never should have dreamed of it. But I knew that the wharf would be a public convenience. If the owner of the stones should build a house with them, nobody would enjoy any advantage but himself. Now, I made use of them in a way that was for the advantage of many persons."

"My son," said Mr. Franklin solemnly, "so far as it was in your power, you have done a greater harm to the public than to the owner of the stones. I do verily believe, Benjamin, that almost all the public and private misery of mankind arises from a neglect of this great truth,—that evil can produce only evil, that good ends must be wrought out by good means."

To the end of his life, Ben Franklin never forgot this conversation with his father; and we have reason to suppose, that, in most of his public and private career, he sought to act upon the principles which that good and wise man then taught him.

Name _____

"Young Benjamin Franklin"— Divided Reading

Monday

When Benjamin Franklin was a boy he was very fond of fishing; and many of his leisure hours were spent on the margin of the mill pond catching flounders, perch, and eels that came up thither with the tide.

The place where Ben and his playmates did most of their fishing was a marshy spot on the outskirts of Boston. On the edge of the water there was a deep bed of clay, in which the boys were forced to stand while they caught their fish.

"This is very uncomfortable," said Ben Franklin one day to his comrades, while they were standing in the quagmire.

"So it is," said the other boys. "What a pity we have no better place to stand!"

Name _____

"Young Benjamin Franklin"— Divided Reading *(cont.)*

Tuesday

On the dry land, not far from the quagmire, there were at that time a great many large stones that had been brought there to be used in building the foundation of a new house. Ben mounted upon the highest of these stones.

"Boys," said he, "I have thought of a plan. You know what a plague it is to have to stand in the quagmire yonder. See, I am bedaubed to the knees, and you are all in the same plight.

"Now I propose that we build a wharf. You see these stones? The workmen mean to use them for building a house here. My plan is to take these same stones, carry them to the edge of the water, and build a wharf with them. What say you, lads? Shall we build the wharf?"

"Yes, yes," cried the boys; "let's set about it!"

It was agreed that they should all be on the spot that evening, and begin their grand public enterprise by moonlight.

Name _____

"Young Benjamin Franklin"— Divided Reading *(cont.)*

Wednesday

Accordingly, at the appointed time, the boys met and eagerly began to remove the stones. They worked like a colony of ants, sometimes two or three of them taking hold of one stone; and at last they had carried them all away, and built their little wharf.

"Now, boys," cried Ben, when the job was done, "let's give three cheers, and go home to bed. To-morrow we may catch fish at our ease."

"Hurrah! hurrah! hurrah!" shouted his comrades, and all scampered off home and to bed, to dream of to-morrow's sport.

In the morning the masons came to begin their work. But what was their surprise to find the stones all gone! The master mason, looking carefully on the ground, saw the tracks of many little feet, some with shoes and some barefoot. Following these to the water side, he soon found what had become of the missing building stones.

"Ah! I see what the mischief is," said he; "those little rascals who were here yesterday have stolen the stones to build a wharf. And I must say that they understand their business well."

Name _____

"Young Benjamin Franklin"— Divided Reading *(cont.)*

Thursday

He was so angry that he at once went to make a complaint before the magistrate; and his Honor wrote an order to "take the bodies of Benjamin Franklin, and other evil-disposed persons," who had stolen a heap of stones.

If the owner of the stolen property had not been more merciful than the master mason, it might have gone hard with our friend Benjamin and his comrades. But, luckily for them, the gentleman had a respect for Ben's father, and, moreover, was pleased with the spirit of the whole affair. He therefore let the culprits off easily.

But the poor boys had to go through another trial, and receive sentence, and suffer punishment, too, from their own fathers. Many a rod was worn to the stump on that unlucky night. As for Ben, he was less afraid of a whipping than of his father's reproof. And, indeed, his father was very much disturbed.

"Benjamin, come hither," began Mr. Franklin in his usual stern and weighty tone. The boy approached and stood before his father's chair.

"Benjamin," said his father, "what could induce you to take property which did not belong to you?"

Name _____

"Young Benjamin Franklin"— Divided Reading *(cont.)*

Friday

"Why, father," replied Ben, hanging his head at first, but then lifting his eyes to Mr. Franklin's face, "if it had been merely for my own benefit, I never should have dreamed of it. But I knew that the wharf would be a public convenience. If the owner of the stones should build a house with them, nobody would enjoy any advantage but himself. Now, I made use of them in a way that was for the advantage of many persons."

"My son," said Mr. Franklin solemnly, "so far as it was in your power, you have done a greater harm to the public than to the owner of the stones. I do verily believe, Benjamin, that almost all the public and private misery of mankind arises from a neglect of this great truth,—that evil can produce only evil, that good ends must be wrought out by good means."

To the end of his life, Ben Franklin never forgot this conversation with his father; and we have reason to suppose, that, in most of his public and private career, he sought to act upon the principles which that good and wise man then taught him.

Name _____

The Life of Benjamin Franklin

Directions: Meet with your group to discuss, research, and answer the questions below.

1. What do you know about Benjamin Franklin?

   _____

   _____

   _____

2. What role did Franklin play in politics?

   _____

   _____

   _____

3. What lesson did Benjamin Franklin learn in Hawthorne's story?

   _____

   _____

   _____

4. How do you think this lesson helped him in his adult life?

   _____

   _____

   _____

   _____

The Federalist Papers

Objective

√ Students will read passages fluently and accurately within a reader's theater activity, focusing on correct conversational, expressive language.

Materials

- copy of *Excerpt from "The Federalist Papers"* (page 183) for the teacher
- copies of *"The Federalist Papers"—Reader's Theater* (pages 184–186) for the students
- copies of *Requirements for President* (page 187) for the students
- video recorder and videotape

Fluency Suggestions and Activities

You may want to complete the history and/or vocabulary activities on the following page before this fluency activity. An understanding of the historical context and vocabulary will help students analyze and read the piece fluently.

1. Explain to the students that the text for this fluency lesson explains the part of the Constitution referring to the office of president. Read the following excerpt to demonstrate fluency. Draw students' attention to your tone of voice, reading rate, accuracy, and expression. Explain that this is a difficult text and that elements of fluency must be used in order to bring better understanding to the audience for which they will perform.

   The power of making treaties is an important one, especially as it relates to war, peace, and commerce; and it should not be delegated but in such a mode, and with such precautions, as will afford the highest security that it will be exercised by men the best qualified for the purpose, and in the manner most conducive to the public good.

2. Explain that this text will be read in a reader's theater format. The text is divided into five parts and each student in a group will be assigned to read each part. Divide the students into groups of five and assign parts to the students. Remind them that the parts are labeled R1 (for Reader 1) through R5. Point out that some parts are labeled "All." These parts are to be read by all students at the same time.

3. Allow the students time in class to practice reading their parts, focusing on expressive, conversational language. When students have had the opportunity to practice reading their parts several times and on a few different occasions, ask them to recite their reader's theater performances for other students in the school. Make a videotape of the students' performances.

4. John Jay is from New York. Find another class from New York and become pen pals with that class. Have students learn all they can about John Jay from their pen pals. Then send the videotape of the students' performances to the pen pals.

The Federalist Papers *(cont.)*

History Connection

Begin the lesson by providing students with background information about "The Federalist Papers." Ask the students if they know any of the requirements of being president of the United States, such as age requirements or citizenship. Then ask them why it might be important to have specific requirements for the person elected to lead the country.

Some people complained about the proposed changes to the Articles of Confederation. Three important men decided to write letters to newspapers in New York. In the letters, they gave reasons why the new Constitution was a good form of government. Their letters, called "The Federalist Papers," made a difference. One by one, the states began to ratify the Constitution.

Vocabulary Connection

Discuss unfamiliar vocabulary encountered in the text. Some possible words are listed below. After identifying the difficult words, discuss them within the context of the text.

- **treaties**—agreements
- **concur**—agree
- **conducive**—helpful
- **electors**—people who vote
- **deputed**—delegated
- **legislatures**—groups of people who make laws
- **zeal**—enthusiasm
- **supineness**—somebody who does not care
- **enlightened**—well informed
- **distinguished**—someone who stands out
- **virtue**—good qualities
- **transient**—something that passes quickly
- **meteors**—small rocks or particles that float in space
- **discretion**—good judgments
- **discernment**—to decide correctly when something is true or false
- **merits**—deserves

Extension Idea

- Divide students into small groups to complete the activity sheet, *Requirements for President* (page 187).

Excerpt from "The Federalist Papers"

FEDERALIST No. 64

By John Jay on Friday, March 7, 1788

To the People of the State of New York:

. . . The second section [of the Constitution] gives power to the President, "BY AND WITH THE ADVICE AND CONSENT OF THE SENATE, TO MAKE TREATIES, PROVIDED TWO THIRDS OF THE SENATORS PRESENT CONCUR."

The power of making treaties is an important one, especially as it relates to war, peace, and commerce; and it should not be delegated but in such a mode, and with such precautions, as will afford the highest security that it will be exercised by men the best qualified for the purpose, and in the manner most conducive to the public good. The convention appears to have been attentive to both these points: they have directed the President to be chosen by select bodies of electors, to be deputed by the people for that express purpose; and they have committed the appointment of senators to the State legislatures. This mode has, in such cases, vastly the advantage of elections by the people in their collective capacity, where the activity of party zeal, taking the advantage of the supineness, the ignorance, and the hopes and fears of the unwary and interested, often places men in office by the votes of a small proportion of the electors.

As the select assemblies for choosing the President, as well as the State legislatures who appoint the senators, will in general be composed of the most enlightened and respectable citizens, there is reason to presume that their attention and their votes will be directed to those men only who have become the most distinguished by their abilities and virtue, and in whom the people perceive just grounds for confidence. The Constitution manifests very particular attention to this object. By excluding men under thirty-five from the first office, and those under thirty from the second, it confines the electors to men of whom the people have had time to form a judgment, and with respect to whom they will not be liable to be deceived by those brilliant appearances of genius and patriotism, which, like transient meteors, sometimes mislead as well as dazzle. If the observation be well founded, that wise kings will always be served by able ministers, it is fair to argue, that as an assembly of select electors possess, in a greater degree than kings, the means of extensive and accurate information relative to men and characters, so will their appointments bear at least equal marks of discretion and discernment. The inference which naturally results from these considerations is this, that the President and senators so chosen will always be of the number of those who best understand our national interests, whether considered in relation to the several States or to foreign nations, who are best able to promote those interests, and whose reputation for integrity inspires and merits confidence. With such men the power of making treaties may be safely lodged.

PUBLIUS.

Name _____

"The Federalist Papers"—
Reader's Theater

All: **To the People of the State of New York: . . . The second section [of the Constitution] gives power to the President, "BY AND WITH THE ADVICE AND CONSENT OF THE SENATE, TO MAKE TREATIES, PROVIDED TWO THIRDS OF THE SENATORS PRESENT CONCUR."**

R1:   The power of making treaties is an important one,

R2:   especially as it relates to war, peace, and commerce;

R3:   and it should not be delegated but in such a mode,

R4:   and with such precautions,

R5:   as will afford the highest security that it will be exercised by men the best qualified for the purpose,

All: **and in the manner most conducive to the public good.**

R1:   The convention appears to have been attentive to both these points:

R2:   they have directed the President to be chosen by select bodies of electors,

R3:   to be designated by the people for that express purpose;

R4:   and they have committed the appointment of senators to the State legislatures.

R5:   This mode has, in such cases, vastly the advantage of elections by the people in their collective capacity,

R1:   where the activity of party zeal,

"The Federalist Papers"— Reader's Theater *(cont.)*

R2: taking the advantage of the laziness, the ignorance, and the hopes and fears of the unwary and interested,

R3: often places men in office by the votes of a small proportion of the electors.

R4: As the select assemblies for choosing the President, as well as the State legislatures who appoint the senators,

R5: will in general be composed of the most enlightened and respectable citizens,

R1: there is reason to presume that their attention and their votes will be directed to those men only

R2: who have become the most distinguished by their abilities and virtue,

R3: and in whom the people perceive just grounds for confidence.

All: **The Constitution manifests very particular attention to this object.**

R4: By excluding men under thirty-five from the first office, and those under thirty from the second,

R5: it confines the electors to men of whom the people have had time to form a judgment,

R1: and with respect to whom they will not be liable to be deceived

R2: by those brilliant appearances of genius and patriotism,

R3: which, like fast-moving meteors, sometimes mislead as well as dazzle.

"The Federalist Papers"— Reader's Theater *(cont.)*

R4:   If the observation be well founded, that wise kings will always be served by able ministers,

R5:   it is fair to argue, that as an assembly of select electors possess,

R1:   in a greater degree than kings,

R2:   the means of extensive and accurate information relative to men and characters,

R3:   so will their appointments bear at least equal marks of discretion and discernment.

R4:   The inference which naturally results from these considerations is this,

R5:   that the President and senators so chosen will always be of the number of those who best understand our national interests,

R1:   whether considered in relation to the several States or to foreign nations,

R2:   who are best able to promote those interests,

R3:   and whose reputation for integrity inspires and merits confidence.

All: **With such men the power of making treaties may be safely lodged.**

Name _____

Requirements for President

Directions: Work with a group of students to discuss and answer the questions below.

1. What is the youngest age a president should be? Oldest? Why do you think this?

    _____

    _____

    _____

2. Is it important that the president be a citizen of the United States? Explain.

    _____

    _____

    _____

3. Do you think a person born in another country should be able to be president if he or she is now a United States citizen? Explain your answer.

    _____

    _____

    _____

4. Should both men and women be allowed to hold the office of president? Why or why not?

    _____

    _____

    _____

    _____

Treaty of Paris Boundaries

Objective

√ Students will determine the meaning of a text and then participate in a public oral reading of the text, focusing on the use of appropriate expression.

Materials

- copies of *Treaty of Paris Boundaries Description* (page 190) for the students
- copies of *Treaty of Paris—Reader's Theater* (page 191) for the students
- copies of *Analyzing the Treaty of Paris* (page 192) for the students
- detailed maps of North America

Fluency Suggestions and Activities

You may want to complete the history and/or vocabulary activities on the following page before this fluency activity. An understanding of the historical context and vocabulary will help students analyze and read the piece fluently.

1. Tell the students that the fluency text for this lesson was written by John Jay who explained to the citizens of New York the boundaries of the agreement of the Treaty of Paris. The students' job in this lesson activity is to read the boundary information aloud as they point out the boundaries on the map.

2. Divide the students into groups of three, providing each student with a copy of the *Treaty of Paris Boundaries Description* (page 190) and the *Treaty of Paris–Reader's Theater* (page 191). Also, provide each student a detailed map of this area. Have the students read the boundaries description written by John Jay and then use their detailed maps to locate the areas described, such as Nova Scotia, the St. Croix River, and the St. Lawrence River on *Analyzing the Treaty of Paris* (page 192). (Allow students to locate some of the bays, rivers, and lakes using the Internet as an alternate source.)

3. When they have finished adding boundaries to the map, have them practice reading their reader's theater scripts. Have the students point to areas on the map as they read their parts. Encourage the students to focus on the accuracy of their reading, as well as on expression and reading rate.

4. After they have practiced reading with fluency, explain that they will need to provide their audiences with background information about the Treaty of Paris, so the audience will better understand their presentations. Encourage them to use reference materials and/or conduct Internet searches to locate this information.

5. Have each group of students work together to write a paragraph or two providing this information. Then have each group determine how this information will be presented (choral reading, individual reading, paired reading, etc.).

6. Arrange to have each group deliver its presentation to other classes in the school, to a group of school administrators and staff members, or to parents.

Treaty of Paris Boundaries *(cont.)*

History Connection

Begin the lesson by explaining to the students that the Treaty of Paris was an agreement that ended the American Revolution. France was required to give land to Great Britain. Then, display the map on page 192. Explain to the students that the shaded area on the map shows the land that was given to the United States in the agreement.

After the war, a treaty was written between Britain and the colonists. The Treaty of Paris was signed in France on September 3, 1783. Benjamin Franklin, John Jay, and John Adams helped lead the talks for the Americans.

The treaty stated that Great Britain had to accept the United States as its own country. Great Britain gave the United States land from the Atlantic Ocean to the Mississippi River. The United States stretched north and south from Canada to Florida. The British had to remove all of their troops from the United States. However, Great Britain was allowed to keep control of French Canada. The American government had to return any land that was taken during the war from British Loyalists. Great Britain was also permitted to continue to use the Mississippi River.

Vocabulary Connection

Discuss unfamiliar vocabulary encountered in the text. Some possible words are listed below. After identifying the difficult words, discuss them within the context of the text.

- **disputes**—arguments
- **hereby**—by this document
- **thence**—from that place
- **latitude**—a unit used to measure the Earth
- **aforesaid**—something that has already been said or named in the document
- **leagues**—a unit used to measure distance

Extension Idea

- Divide students into small groups to discuss the map of the Treaty of Paris. Have them work together to identify the modern-day states that make up this area today. Also, have them discuss how the United States might be different today, if this area had remained under the ownership of Great Britain.

Treaty of Paris Boundaries Description

And that all disputes which might arise in future on the subject of the boundaries of the said United States may be prevented, it is hereby agreed and declared, that the following are and shall be their boundaries:

- from the northwest angle of Nova Scotia, that angle which is formed by a line drawn due north from the source of St. Croix River to the highlands
- along the said highlands which divide those rivers that empty themselves into the river St. Lawrence, from those which fall into the Atlantic Ocean, to the northwesternmost head of Connecticut River
- thence down along the middle of that river to the forty-fifth degree of north latitude
- from thence by a line due west on said latitude until it strikes the river Iroquois or Cataraquy
- thence along the middle of said river into Lake Ontario
- through the middle of said lake until it strikes the communication by water between that lake and Lake Erie
- thence along the middle of said communication into Lake Erie, through the middle of said lake until it arrives at the water communication between that lake and Lake Huron
- thence along the middle of said water communication into Lake Huron, thence through the middle of said lake to the water communication between that lake and Lake Superior
- thence through Lake Superior northward of the Isles Royal and Phelipeaux to the Long Lake
- thence through the middle of said Long Lake and the water communication between it and the Lake of the Woods, to the said Lake of the Woods
- thence through the said lake to the most northwesternmost point thereof, and from thence on a due west course to the river Mississippi
- thence by a line to be drawn along the middle of the said river Mississippi until it shall intersect the northernmost part of the thirty-first degree of north latitude, South, by a line to be drawn due east from the determination of the line last mentioned in the latitude of thirty-one degrees of the equator, to the middle of the river Apalachicola or Catahouche
- thence along the middle thereof to its junction with the Flint River
- thence straight to the head of Saint Mary's River
- thence down along the middle of Saint Mary's River to the Atlantic Ocean
- east, by a line to be drawn along the middle of the river Saint Croix, from its mouth in the Bay of Fundy to its source, and from its source directly north to the aforesaid highlands which divide the rivers that fall into the Atlantic Ocean from those which fall into the river Saint Lawrence
- comprehending all islands within twenty leagues of any part of the shores of the United States, and lying between lines to be drawn due east from the points where the aforesaid boundaries between Nova Scotia on the one part and East Florida on the other shall, respectively, touch the Bay of Fundy and the Atlantic Ocean, excepting such islands as now are or heretofore have been within the limits of the said province of Nova Scotia

Name _____

Treaty of Paris—Reader's Theater

R1:   Start at the northwest angle of Nova Scotia and draw a line due north from the source of St. Croix River to the highlands.

R2:   Then, draw a line along the highlands to the northwesternmost head of Connecticut River.

R3:   Next, draw a line down the middle of that river to the 45th degree of north latitude.

R1:   From there draw a line due west on the 45th line of latitude until it strikes the river Iroquois or Cataraquy.

R2:   Again, draw a line down the middle of the river into Lake Ontario.

R3:   Continue through the middle of the lake until you reach the water connection between that lake and Lake Erie.

R1:   Next, go along the middle of the connection with Lake Erie, into the middle of the lake until the water connection between that lake and Lake Huron.

R2:   Then, continue along the middle of the water connection between the lakes and through the middle of Lake Huron to the water connection between that lake and Lake Superior.

R3:   Go through Lake Superior northward of the Isles Royal and Phelipeaux to the Long Lake.

R1:   Then, continue through the middle of Long Lake and the water communication between it and the Lake of the Woods.

R2:   Next, go through the Lake of the Woods to the most northwesternmost point and from there travel due west to the Mississippi River.

R3:   Draw a line down the middle of the Mississippi Rivier until you meet the 31st degree of north latitude.

R1:   Continue with a line to be drawn due east from the last line to the middle of the river Apalachicola or Catahouche.

R2:   Then, go along the middle of that river to its junction with the Flint River.

R3:   Continue straight ahead to the head of Saint Mary's River.

R1:   Next, continue down along the middle of Saint Mary's River to the Atlantic Ocean.

R2:   Draw a line along the middle of the river Saint Croix, from its mouth in the Bay of Fundy to its source, and from its source directly north to the aforesaid highlands.

R3:   This includes all islands within 20 leagues of any part of the shores of the United States and lying between lines to be drawn due east from the points where the aforesaid boundaries between Nova Scotia on the one part and East Florida on the other shall touch the Bay of Fundy and the Atlantic Ocean.

Name _____

Analyzing the Treaty of Paris

Directions: This map shows all the land belonging to the United States in 1783. Label the map according to the instructions below.

1. Find Nova Scotia and label it on the map above.

2. Label the following rivers: St. Croix River, St. Lawrence River, Connecticut River, Iroquois River, Apalachicola River, Flint River, Saint Mary's River, and the Mississippi River.

3. Label the following lakes: Lake Ontario, Lake Erie, Lake Huron, Lake Superior, Long Lake, and the Lake of the Woods.

4. Label the Atlantic Ocean.

5. Find and label the following: Isles Royal, Bay of Fundy, and Florida.

Note: The isle of Phelipeaux is mentioned in the Treaty of Paris. This "isle" was included on a map of Lake Superior created in 1744, but it actually does not exist.